Transportation

CONTROLLED ACCESS HIGHWAYS

	Free
Toll	Toll; Toll Booth
	Under Construction
1 12	Interchange and Exit Number
	Ramp Downtown maps only
® ® ⓢ	Rest Area; Service Area Yellow with facilities

OTHER HIGHWAYS

	Primary Highway
	Secondary Highway
	Multilane Divided Highway Primary and secondary highways only
	Other Paved Road
	Unpaved Road Check conditions locally

HIGHWAY MARKERS

12	Interstate Route
12	U.S. Route
12	State or Provincial Route
12 A A12	County or Other Route
BUS 12 BUS 12	Business Route
12	Trans-Canada Highway
12	Canadian Provincial Autoroute
12	Mexican Federal Route

OTHER SYMBOLS

12	Distances along Major Highways Miles in U.S.; kilometers in Canada and Mexico
)(	Tunnel; Pass
··········	Scenic Drive
⊗	Wayside Stop
→	One-way Street
⤧	Port of Entry
✈	Airport
-------	Auto Ferry; Passenger Ferry

Recreation and Features of Interest

	National Park
	Forest, Grassland, or BLM Recreation Area
	Other Large Park or Recreation Area
👥 👤	Small State Park with and without Camping
⌂	Public Campsite
-------	Trail
▪	Point of Interest
ⓘ	Visitor Information Center
⛳ ⛳	Public Golf Course; Private Golf Course Professional tournament location; city maps only
✚	Hospital City maps only
⛷	Ski Area

Cities and Towns

✪ ⊛	National Capital; State or Provincial Capital
◉	County Seat State maps only
●	Cities, Towns, and Populated Places Type size indicates relative importance
	Urban Area State and province maps only
	Large Incorporated Cities City maps only

Other Map Features

JEFFERSON	County Boundary and Name
40°N 95°W	Latitude; Longitude
	Time Zone Boundary
+ Mt. Olympus 7,965	Mountain Peak; Elevation Feet in U.S.; meters in Canada and Mexico
	Perennial; Intermittent River
	Perennial; Intermittent or Dry Water Body
	Dam
	Swamp
	Glacier National Park maps only
DC 52 44	More detailed map is available for this area on page number shown

MAPQUEST®

Road Atlas

UNITED STATES • CANADA • MEXICO

Page Numbers

MapQuest, Inc. is the publisher of this atlas. The information contained herein is derived from a variety of third party sources. While every effort has been made to verify the information contained in such sources, the publisher assumes no responsibility for inconsistencies or inaccuracies in the data nor liability for any damages of any type arising from errors or omissions. Reproduction or recording of any maps, tables, text, or other material contained in this publication in any manner including, without limitation, by photocopying and electronic storage and retrieval, is prohibited.

Copyright © MMVII
by MapQuest, Inc.
All rights reserved.
Printed in Canada

ISBN-10: 1-57262-715-8
ISBN-13: 978-1-57262-715-4

Comments and suggestions:
Managing Editor
MapQuest Road Atlas
MapQuest, Inc.
P.O. Box 601
Mountville, PA 17554-0601
e-mail at roadatlas@mapquest.com
1.800.626.4655

we help people find places

Map Scale
1 : 1,215,000
1 inch = 19.2 miles
or 30.9 kilometers

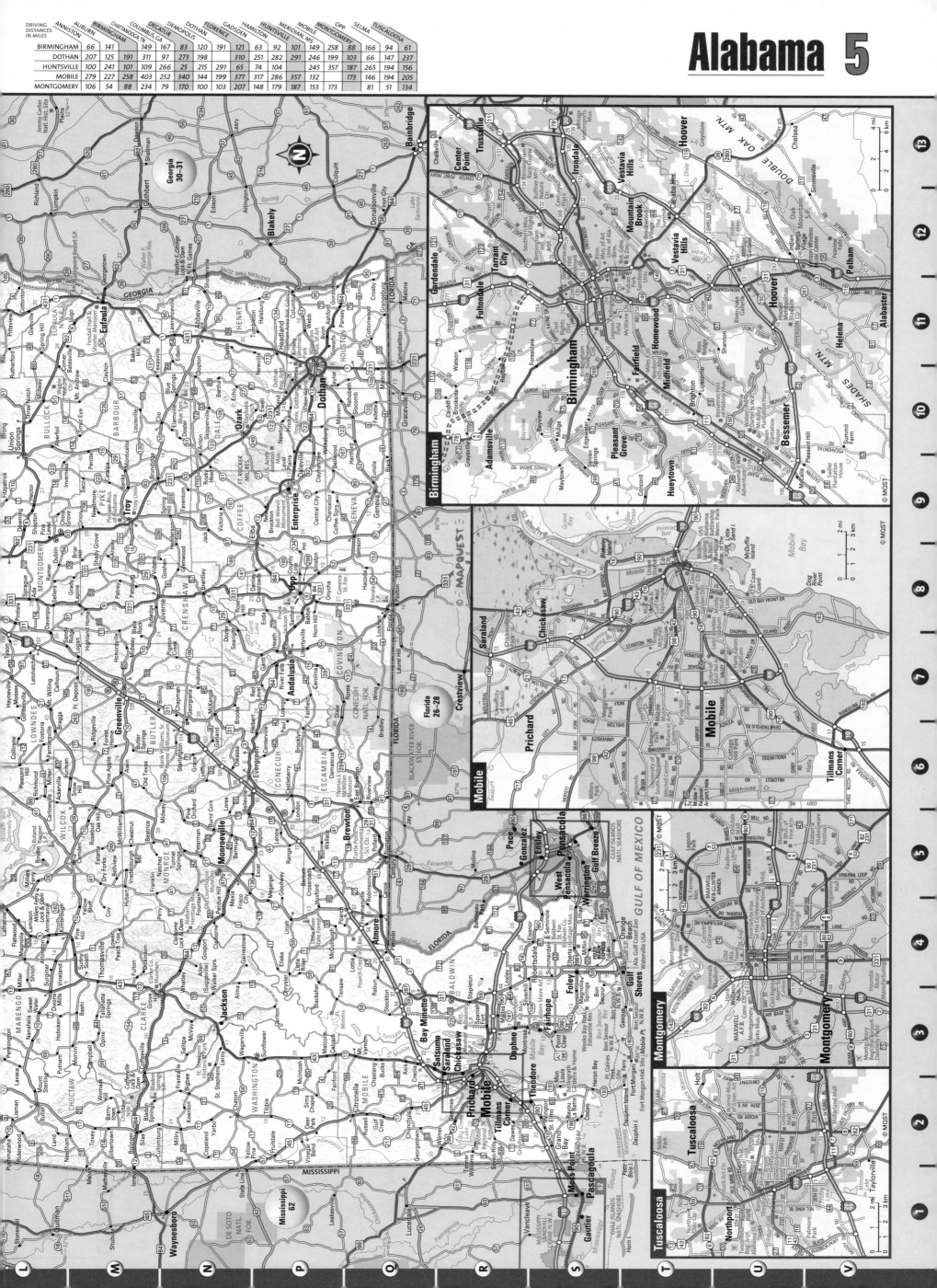

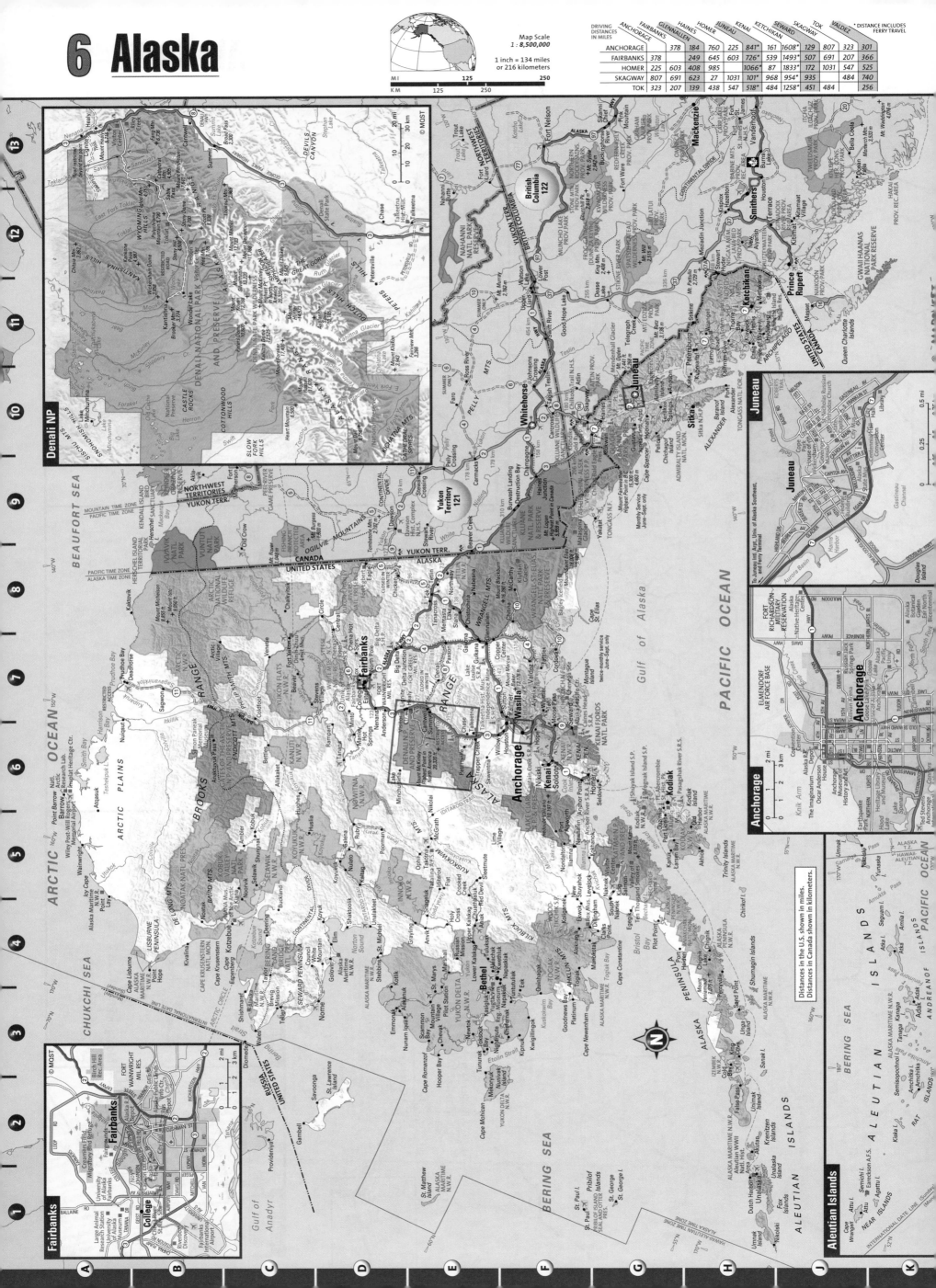

Map Scale
1 : 1,721,000

1 inch = 27.2 miles
or 43.8 kilometers

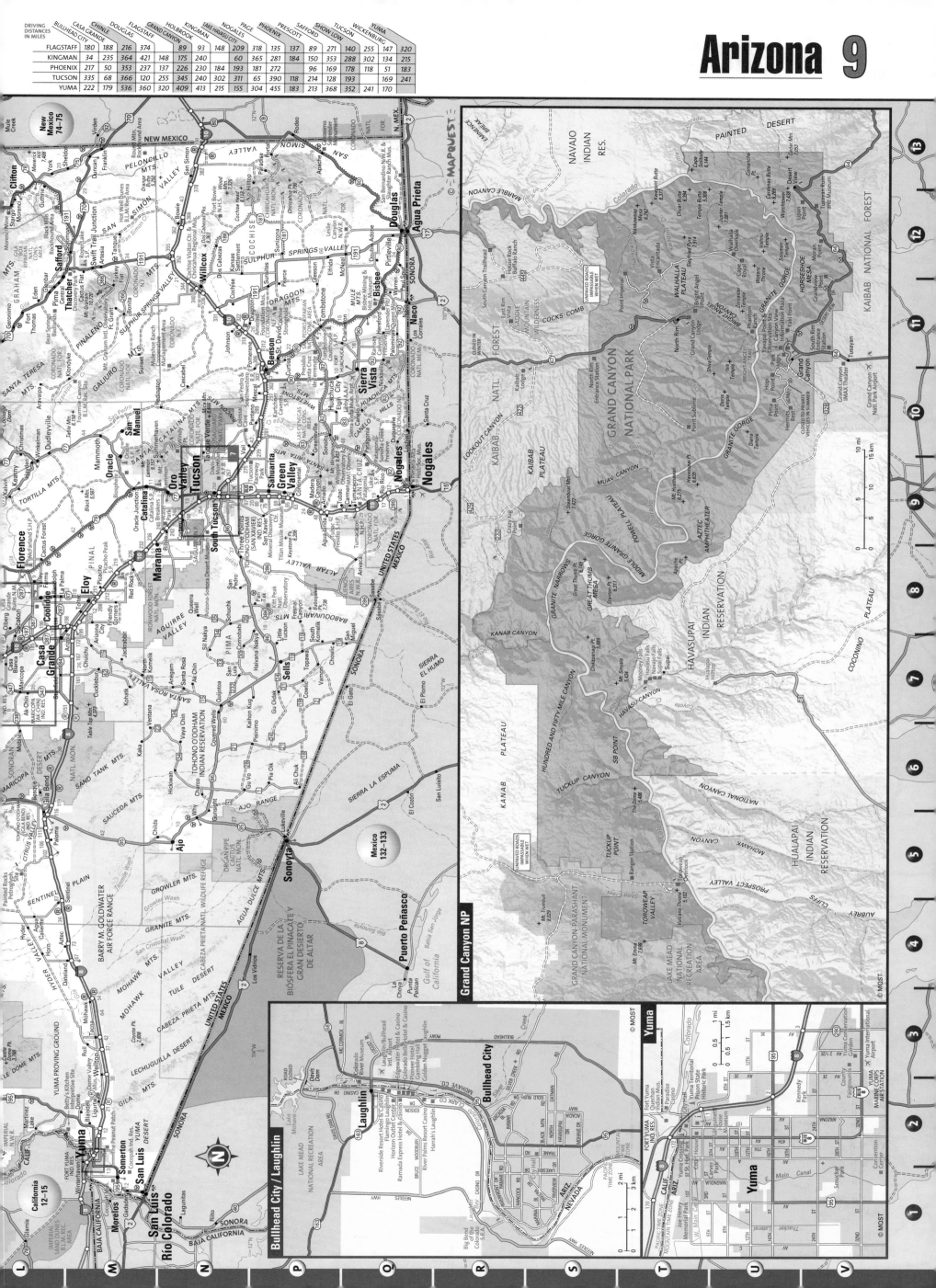

DRIVING DISTANCES IN MILES

	BLYTHEVILLE	CAMDEN	CONWAY	DUMAS	EL DORADO	FAYETTEVILLE	FORT SMITH	HARRISON	HELENA	HOT SPRINGS	JONESBORO	LITTLE ROCK	MEMPHIS, TN	MENA	NEWPORT	PINE BLUFF	RUSSELLVILLE	TEXARKANA
FORT SMITH	353	201	134	255	232	64		141	280	126	266	165	298	81	220	210	87	180
JONESBORO	53	236	133	185	253	287	266	178	111	200		135	70	276	46	180	182	288
LITTLE ROCK	195	101	31	90	118	186	165	136	122	65	135		140	141	89	45	81	153
PINE BLUFF	213	76	76	45	93	231	210	181	106	79	180	45	157	151	134		126	163
TEXARKANA	347	90	176	208	88	244	180	281	273	117	288	153	291	99	241	163	180	

TRAVEL NOTE: California has started numbering freeway exits using a mileage-based numbering system (shown here). Full implementation is expected to take several years.

Monterey Bay

PACIFIC OCEAN

Monterey Bay

© MQST

© MapQuest

DRIVING DISTANCES IN MILES	BISHOP	CHICO	EUREKA	FRESNO	MERCED	MONTEREY	NAPA	OAKLAND	REDDING	SACRAMENTO	SAN FRANCISCO	SAN JOSE	SANTA ROSA	SOUTH LAKE TAHOE	STOCKTON	SUSANVILLE	UKIAH	YOSEMITE VILLAGE
EUREKA	537	186		444	385	380	235	262	133	278	263	306	220	379	336	247	148	436
REDDING	426	74	133	344	284	323	193	213		166	222	250	228	266	214	114	193	336
SACRAMENTO	260	88	278	178	118	188	58	78	166		87	115	93	100	48	183	153	170
SAN FRANCISCO	283	182	263	190	131	114	47	9	222	87		43	56	185	82	277	116	183
SOUTH LAKE TAHOE	179	165	379	267	208	286	156	176	266	100	185	213	191		142	146	251	180

Nevada 70

Bakersfield

San Diego

Downtown San Diego

TRAVEL NOTE: California has started numbering freeway exits using a mileage-based numbering system (shown here). Full implementation is expected to take several years.

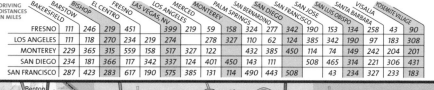

DRIVING DISTANCES IN MILES	BAKERSFIELD	BARSTOW	BISHOP	EL CENTRO	FRESNO	LAS VEGAS, NV	LOS ANGELES	MERCED	MONTEREY	PALM SPRINGS	SAN BERNARDINO	SAN DIEGO	SAN FRANCISCO	SAN JOSE	SAN LUIS OBISPO	SANTA BARBARA	VISALIA	YOSEMITE VILLAGE
FRESNO	111	246	219	451		399	219	59	158	324	277	342	190	153	134	258	43	90
LOS ANGELES	111	118	270	234	219	274		278	327	110	62	124	385	342	190	97	183	308
MONTEREY	229	365	315	559	158	517	327	122		432	385	450	114	74	149	242	204	201
SAN DIEGO	234	181	366	117	342	337	124	401	450	143	111		508	314	221	306	431	
SAN FRANCISCO	287	423	283	617	190	575	385	131	114	490	443	508		43	234	327	233	183

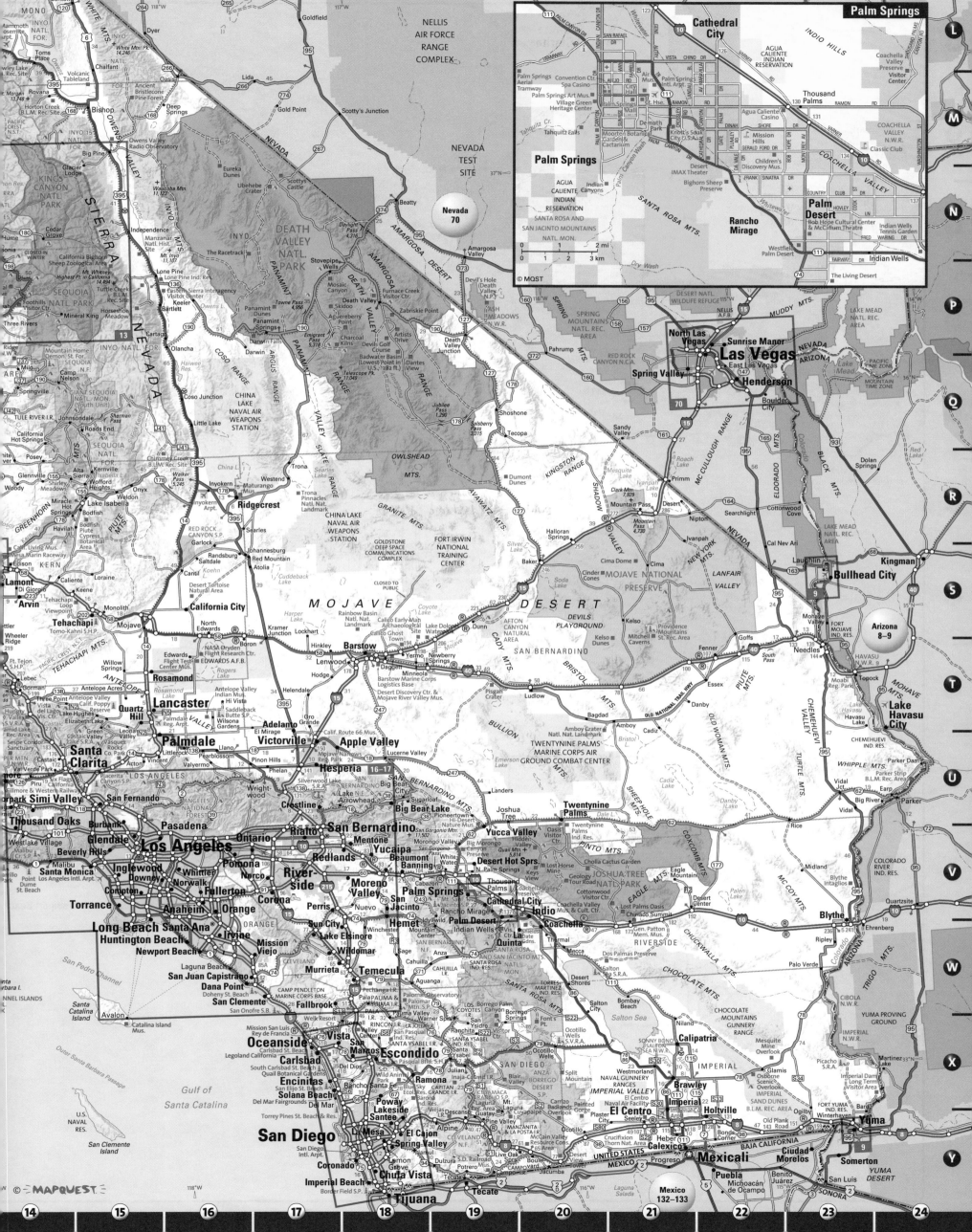

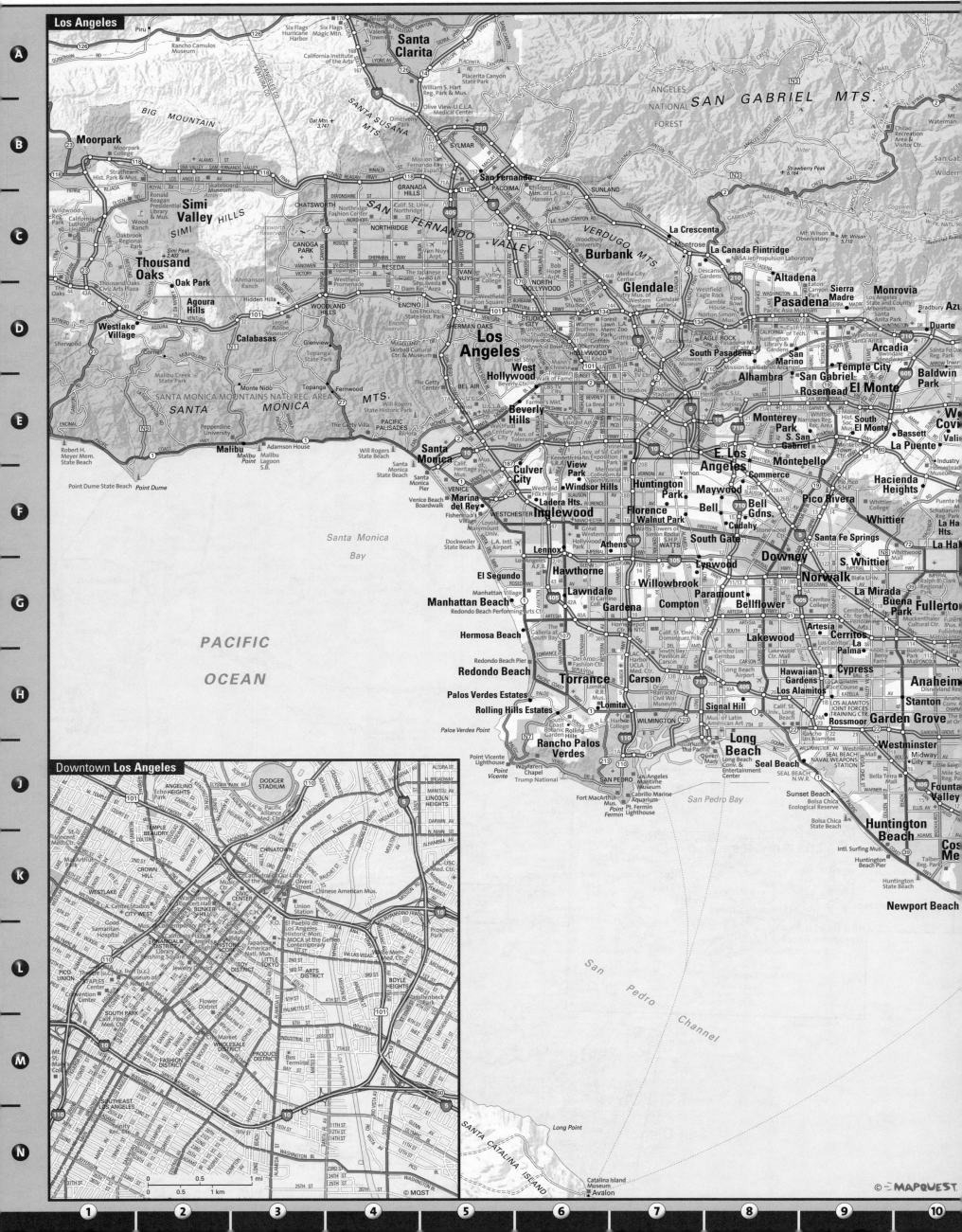

Map Scale
1 : 1,531,000

1 inch = 24.2 miles
or 38.9 kilometers

DRIVING DISTANCES IN MILES	ALAMOSA	ASPEN	BOULDER	BURLINGTON	COLORADO SPRINGS	CRAIG	DENVER	DURANGO	ESTES PARK	FORT COLLINS	GLENWOOD SPRINGS	GRAND JUNCTION	GREELEY	LAMAR	MONTROSE	PUEBLO	STERLING	TRINIDAD
COLORADO SPRINGS	162	157	97	152		270	70	314	134	133	226	318	133	161	236	43	194	127
DENVER	230	164	27	168	70	203		337	64	64	158	250	64	208	277	111	130	196
DURANGO	152	244	366	461	314	321	337		402	399	226	169	399	354	107	271	465	260
GRAND JUNCTION	261	135	254	418	318	152	250	169	291	311	92		311	399	62	360	377	444
PUEBLO	119	185	139	191	43	312	111	271	175	175	268	360	175	119	229		236	84

DRIVING DISTANCES IN MILES	BRIDGEPORT	DANBURY	HARTFORD	MERIDEN	MIDDLETOWN	NEW HAVEN	NEW LONDON	NEW YORK, NY	NORWICH	PROVIDENCE	PUTNAM	SPRINGFIELD, MA	STAMFORD	STORRS	TORRINGTON	WATERBURY	WILLIMANTIC	WINDSOR LOCKS
BRIDGEPORT		31	56	37	44	19	64	60	72	118	100	81	21	75	54	33	79	68
HARTFORD	56	57		21	16	39	46	115	38	73	46	25	77	21	25	30	25	13
NEW LONDON	64	81	46	50	40	46		124	15	58	51	71	85	41	72	65	29	59
TORRINGTON	54	40	25	40	40	50	72	107	64	98	71	50	74	46		21	51	38
WATERBURY	33	31	30	20	25	30	65	99	60	118	76	55	53	51	21		56	43

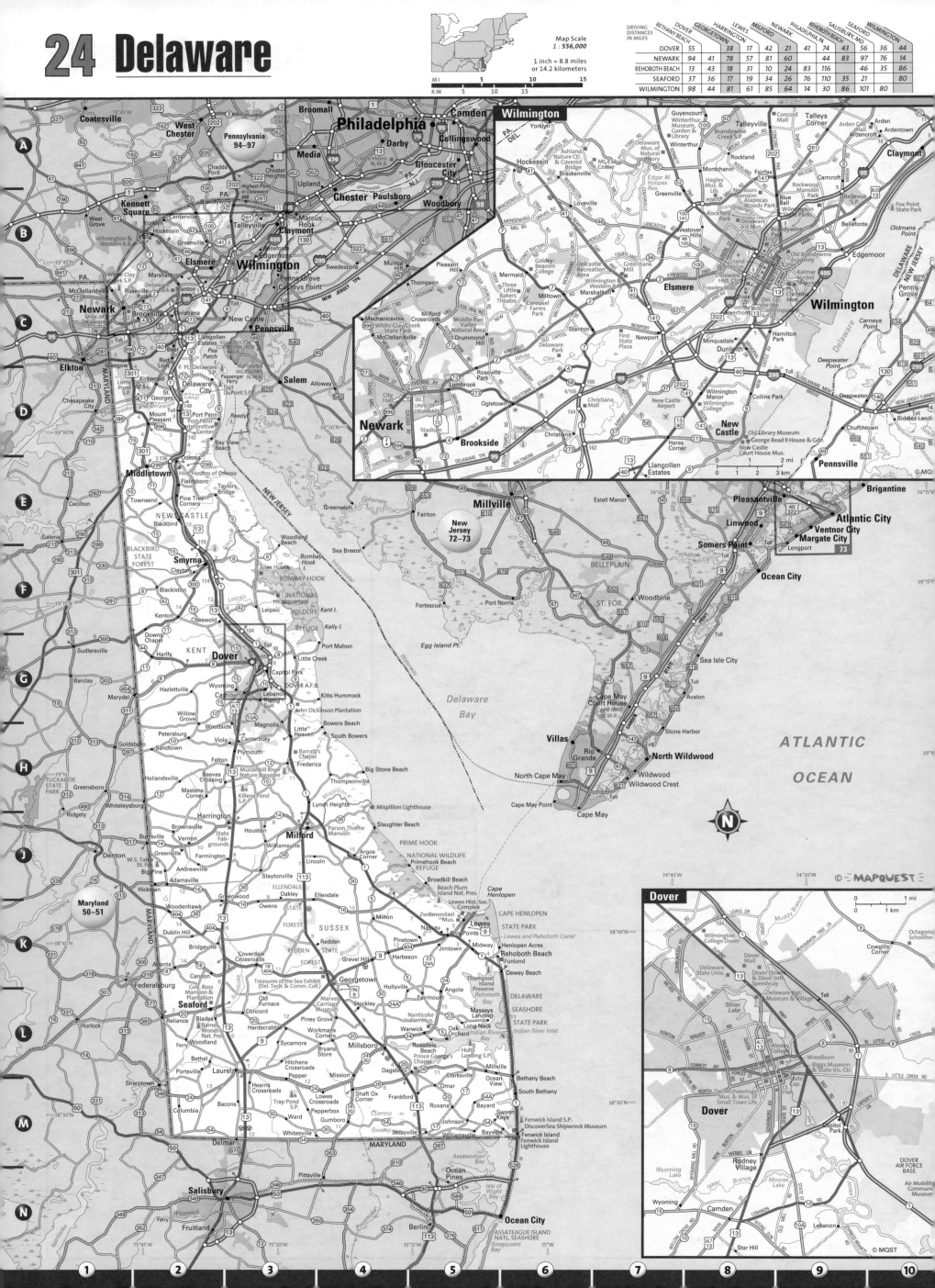

Map Scale
1 : 556,000

1 inch = 8.8 miles
or 14.2 kilometers

© MAPQUEST

Map Scale
1 : 1,465,000

1 inch = 23.1 miles
or 37.2 kilometers

MI 20 40
KM 20 40

Pensacola

Panama City

Tallahasse

Orlando

Jacksonville

GULF OF MEXICO

© MQST

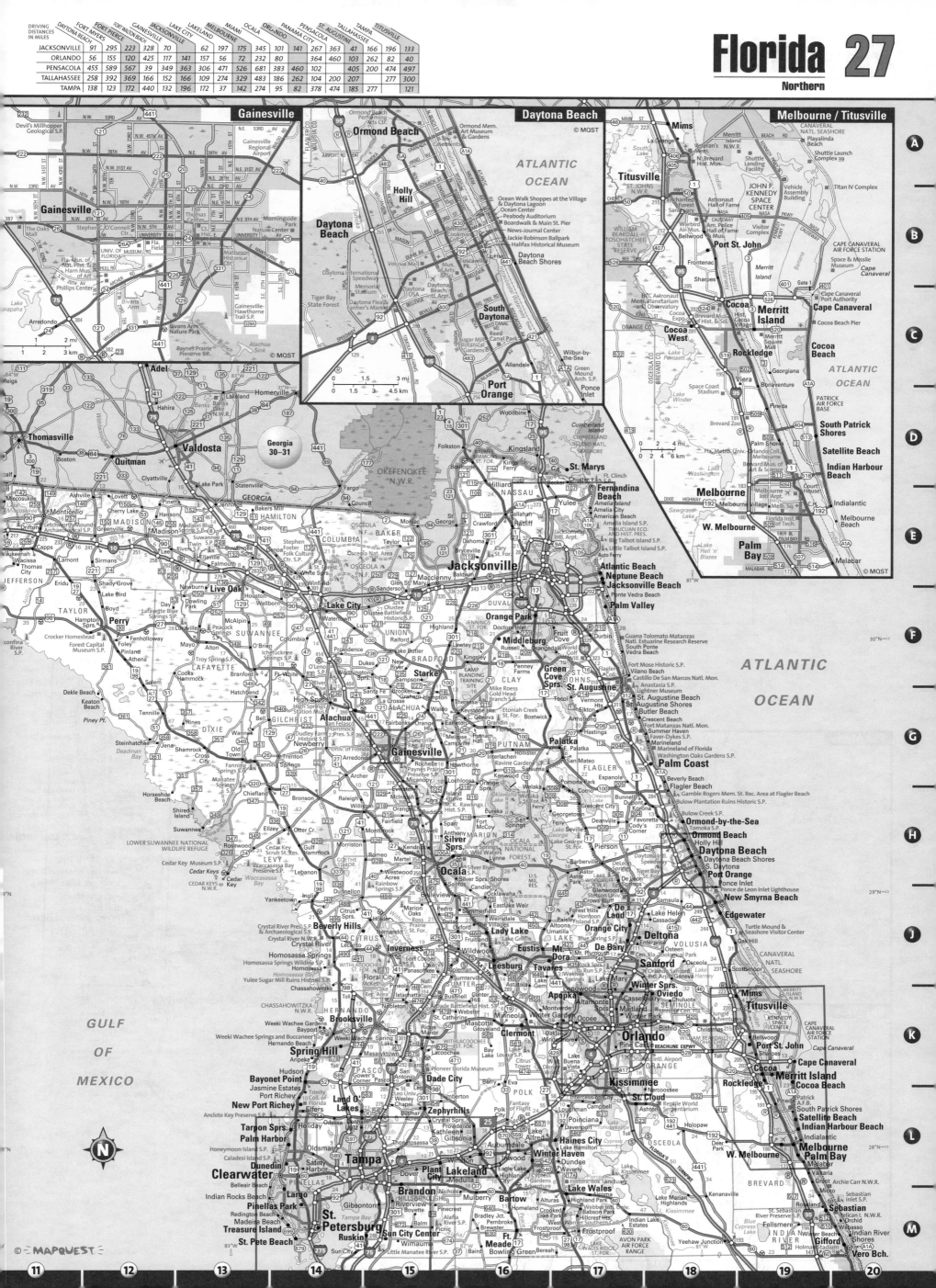

28 Florida
Southern

Map Scale
1 : 1,465,000

1 inch = 23.1 miles
or 37.2 kilometers

DRIVING DISTANCES IN MILES	FORT LAUDERDALE	FORT MYERS	FORT PIERCE	KEY WEST	LAKELAND	MELBOURNE	MIAMI	ORLANDO	ST. PETERSBURG	SARASOTA	TAMPA	WEST PALM BEACH
FORT MYERS	139		126	308	113	178	155	155	108	74	123	125
FORT PIERCE	102	126		288	122	57	122	120	197	150	172	57
MIAMI	23	155	122	168	236	179		232	259	225	274	67
ORLANDO	216	155	120	398	56	72	232		107	130	82	169
TAMPA	257	123	172	426	37	142	274	82	25	60		223

Fort Myers

Key West

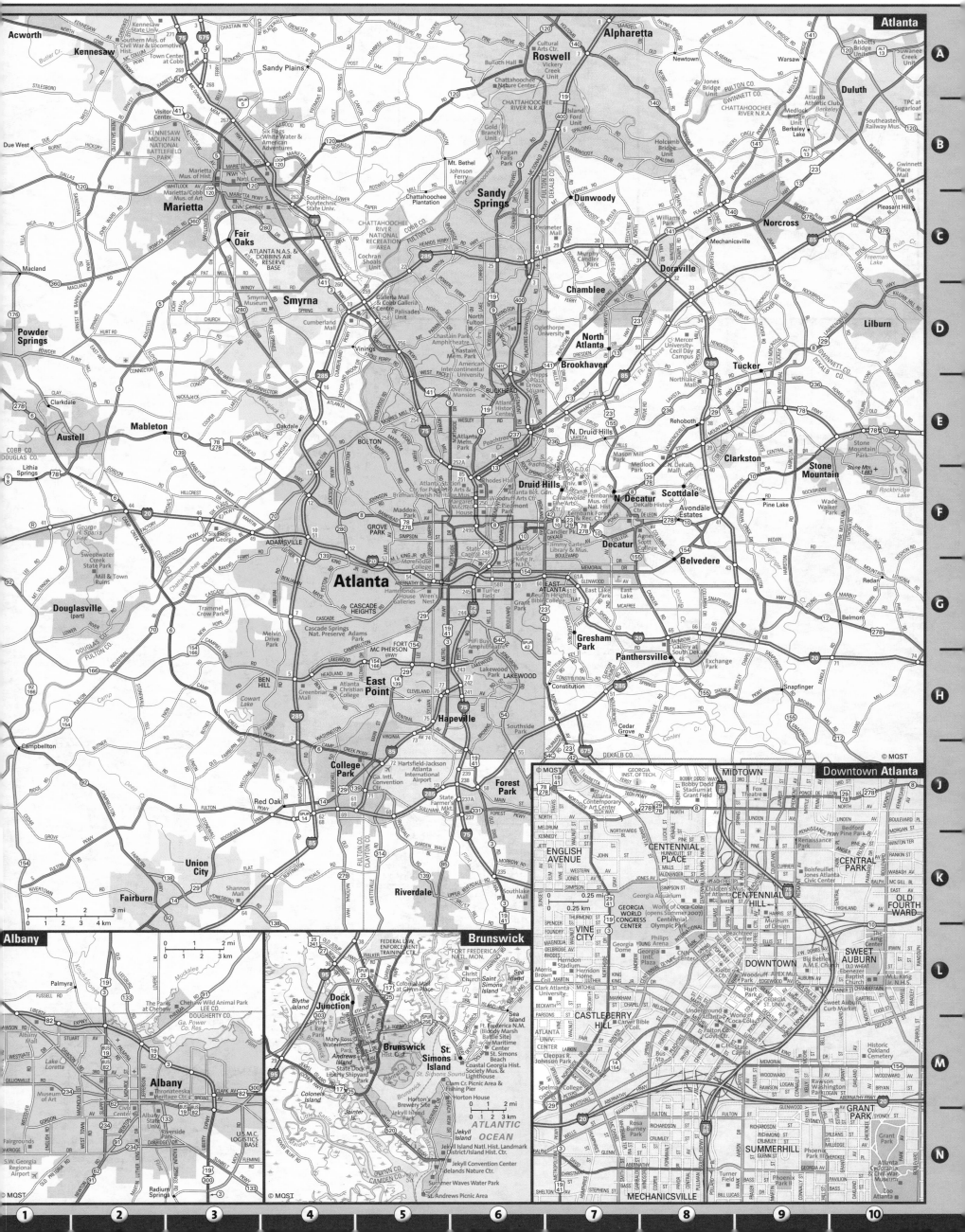

Atlanta

Downtown Atlanta

Albany

Brunswick

© MQST

Map Scale
1 : 1,383,000

1 inch = 21.8 miles
or 35.1 kilometers

DRIVING DISTANCES IN MILES	HĀNA	HILO	HONOLULU	HO'OLEHUA	KAHULUI	KAILUA	KAILUA-KONA	LAHAINA	LĀNA'I CITY	LĪHU'E	WAHIAWĀ	WAIMEA	* DISTANCE INCLUDES AIR TRAVEL
HILO	149*		217*	169*	121*	235*	88	142*	155*	319*	234*	54	
HONOLULU	129*	217*		54*	101*	14	185*	92*	74*	102*	23	172*	
KAHULUI	42	121*	101*	76*		119*	109*	23	57*	202*	118*	79*	
KAILUA-KONA	137*	88	185*	157*	109*	203*		132*	143*	285*	202*	39	
LĪHU'E	230*	319*	102*	156*	202*	120*	285*	225*	176*		119*	174*	

Boise

Pocatello

Idaho Falls

Map Scale
1 : 2,407,000

1 inch = 38.0 miles
or 61.2 kilometers

DRIVING DISTANCES IN MILES	BOISE	COEUR D'ALENE	GRANGEVILLE	IDAHO FALLS	KETCHUM	LEWISTON	MISSOULA MT	MOUNTAIN HOME	POCATELLO	SALMON	SANDPOINT	TWIN FALLS
BOISE		406	202	288	163	270	374	49	241	247	452	134
COEUR D'ALENE	406		186	476	485	118	167	499	526	307	48	584
IDAHO FALLS	288	476	483		153	532	311	240	53	168	523	162
LEWISTON	270	118	74	532		477	221	363	555	337	166	448
POCATELLO	241	526	440	53	190	555	360	193		217	572	116

DRIVING DISTANCES IN MILES	CAIRO	BLOOMINGTON	CARBONDALE	CHAMPAIGN	CHICAGO	DECATUR	DUBUQUE, IA	EFFINGHAM	GALESBURG	JOLIET	KANKAKEE	MOUNT VERNON	PEORIA	QUINCY	ROCKFORD	ROCK ISLAND	ST. LOUIS, MO	SPRINGFIELD
CHAMPAIGN	54	241	199		141	52	263	77	141	115	79	145	94	197	189	191	179	87
CHICAGO	135	376	334	141		186	180	212	198	40	61	280	168	306	86	169	294	197
ROCKFORD	134	424	382	189	86	184	93	260	153	99	139	328	135	272		124	293	196
ST. LOUIS, MO	160	156	105	179	294	116	342	103	220	257	252	81	172	131	293	270		97
SPRINGFIELD	63	254	182	87	197	40	245	89	123	160	152	158	75	110	196	173	97	

Map Scale
1 : 935,000

1 inch = 14.8 miles
or 23.8 kilometers

DRIVING DISTANCES IN MILES	ANDERSON	BLOOMINGTON	COLUMBUS	CRAWFORDSVILLE	EVANSVILLE	FORT WAYNE	GARY	GREENSBURG	INDIANAPOLIS	KOKOMO	LAFAYETTE	LOUISVILLE KY	MUNCIE	PLYMOUTH	RICHMOND	SOUTH BEND	TERRE HAUTE	VINCENNES
EVANSVILLE	211	117	175	164		296	324	195	166	219	194	114	228	281	241	305	107	51
FORT WAYNE	86	175	169	163	296		143	149	128	85	116	236	75	65	95	79	207	253
GARY	180	192	200	122	324	143		210	153	127	91	268	198	66	226	62	161	268
INDIANAPOLIS	43	47	45	47	166	128	153	55		52	66	112	61	114	74	138	77	123
SOUTH BEND	129	187	187	136	305	79	62	187	138	86	104	255	141	24	172		217	263

Map Scale
1 : 1,111,000

1 inch = 17.5 miles
or 28.2 kilometers

DRIVING DISTANCES IN MILES	AMES	BURLINGTON	CARROLL	CEDAR RAPIDS	COUNCIL BLUFFS	CRESTON	DAVENPORT	DECORAH	DES MOINES	DUBUQUE	FORT DODGE	IOWA CITY	MARSHALLTOWN	MASON CITY	OTTUMWA	SIOUX CITY	SPENCER	WATERLOO
COUNCIL BLUFFS	165	323	101	261		99	303	347	130	327	160	245	181	258	216	101	157	238
DES MOINES	34	157	90	129	130	81	171	215		196	94	113	49	126	86	202	188	106
IOWA CITY	136	82	195	28	245	195	59	131	113	84	196		98	173	83	316	267	78
SIOUX CITY	171	394	105	332	101	189	375	303	202	316	120	316	252	218	287		103	228
WATERLOO	95	157	160	53	238	189	137	79	106	93	108	78	58	79	125	228	189	

DRIVING DISTANCES IN MILES	ARKANSAS CITY	ATCHISON	COLBY	DODGE CITY	EMPORIA	GARDEN CITY	GREAT BEND	HAYS	HUTCHINSON	INDEPENDENCE	IOLA	KANSAS CITY	LAWRENCE	LIBERAL	MANHATTAN	SALINA	TOPEKA	WICHITA
DODGE CITY	141	107	315		238	52	83	106	120	270	264	333	298	83	232	164	271	153
KANSAS CITY	247	50	369	333	106	373	250	261	240	162	105		35	402	117	172	61	192
SALINA	151	160	200	164	118	204	81	93	68	206	187	132	137	247	72		111	92
TOPEKA	193	49	308	271	58	311	188	200	178	135	100	61	26	347	55	111		137
WICHITA	61	186	289	153	85	205	119	181	51	118	112	192	159	210	131	92	137	

Map Scale
1 : 1,084,000

1 inch = 17.1 miles
or 27.5 kilometers

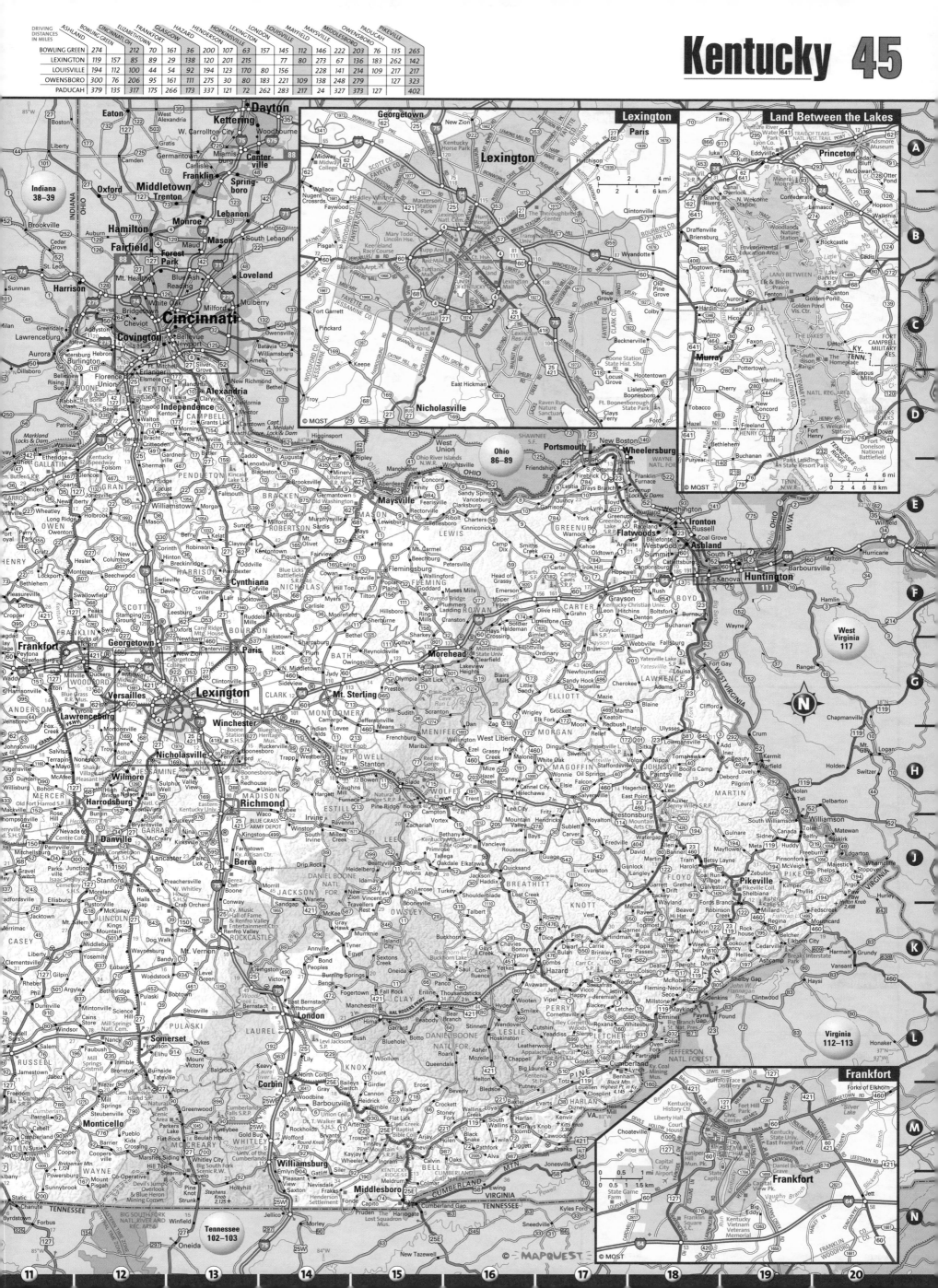

	ASHLAND	BOWLING GREEN	CINCINNATI, OH	ELIZABETHTOWN	FRANKFORT	GLASGOW	HAZARD	HENDERSON	HOPKINSVILLE	LEXINGTON	LONDON	LOUISVILLE	MAYFIELD	MIDDLESBORO	OWENSBORO	PADUCAH	PIKEVILLE
BOWLING GREEN	274		212	70	161	36	200	107	63	157	145	112	146	222	203	76	135	265
LEXINGTON	119	157	85	89	29	138	120	201	215		77	80	273	67	136	183	262	142
LOUISVILLE	194	107	100	44	54	92	194	123	70	80	156		170	141	214	109	217	217
OWENSBORO	300	76	206	95	161	111	275	30	80	183	221	109	138	248		127	127	323
PADUCAH	379	135	317	175	266	173	337	121	72	262	283	217	24	327	373	127		402

Map Scale
1 : 1,000,000

1 inch = 15.8 miles
or 25.4 kilometers

DRIVING DISTANCES IN MILES	AUGUSTA	BANGOR	BAR HARBOR	BRUNSWICK	CALAIS	FARMINGTON	FORT KENT	GREENVILLE	HOULTON	LEWISTON	MACHIAS	MILLINOCKET	PORTLAND	PORTSMOUTH, NH	PRESQUE ISLE	ROCKLAND	SACO	WATERVILLE
AUGUSTA		77	120	32	173	65	269	99	196	35	161	149	58	110	236	43	74	20
BANGOR	77		45	106	97	80	195	74	122	108	85	75	131	184	162	58	147	56
CALAIS	173	97		112	203	177	189	160	91	205	55	228	281	133	155	244	153
HOULTON	196	122	166	226	91	200	98	155		228	126	73	251	304	42	182	267	176
PORTLAND	58	131	175	27	228	81	324	153	251	36	216	203		53	291	78	16	84

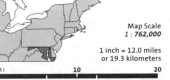

Map Scale
1 : 762,000

1 inch = 12.0 miles
or 19.3 kilometers

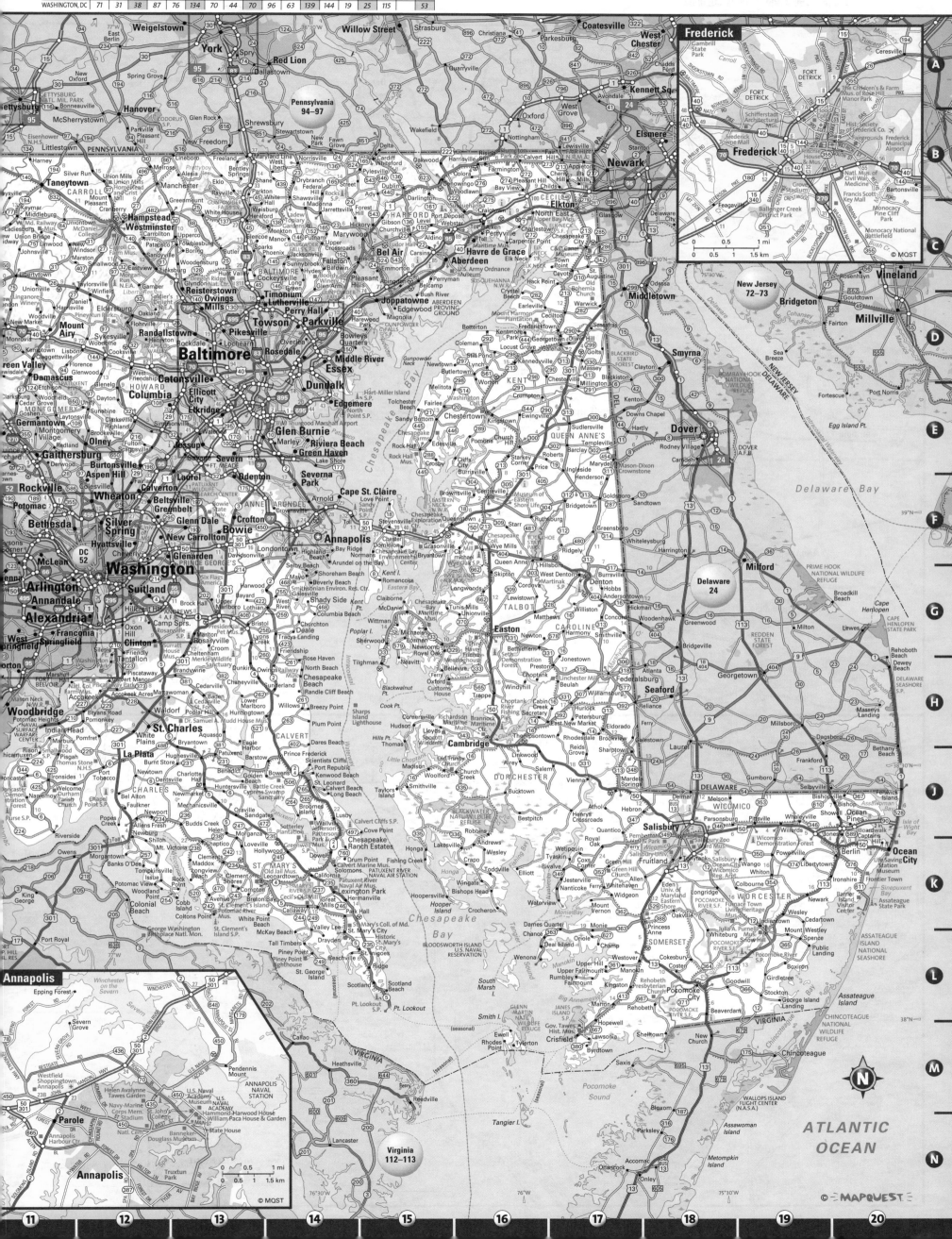

Driving Distances in Miles

	ABERDEEN	ANNAPOLIS	BALTIMORE	CAMBRIDGE	CHESTERTOWN	CUMBERLAND	EASTON	FREDERICK	HAGERSTOWN	HANCOCK	LEXINGTON PARK	OCEAN CITY	POCOMOKE CITY	ROCKVILLE	ST. CHARLES	SALISBURY	WASHINGTON, DC	WESTMINSTER
ANNAPOLIS	54		25	55	45	162	38	73	98	124	66	108	112	47	47	83	31	56
BALTIMORE	35	25		78	68	140	61	51	76	102	95	131	135	45	57	106	38	39
HAGERSTOWN	109	98	76	153	143	67	136	28		29	142	206	211	54	103	182	70	50
SALISBURY	124	83	106	32	81	246	47	156	182	207	70	30	29	130	130		115	138
WASHINGTON, DC	71	31	38	87	76	134	70	44	70	96	63	139	144	19	25	115		53

© MQST

ATLANTIC OCEAN

© MapQuest

Downtown Boston

ATLANTIC OCEAN

Massachusetts Bay

Beverly
Beverly Harbor
Peabody
Salem
Marblehead
Swampscott
Lynn
Saugus
Melrose
Wakefield
Reading
Wilmington
Lynnfield
Essex
Pinehurst
Burlington
Bedford
Woburn
Stoneham
Winchester
Lexington
Arlington
Medford
Malden
Everett
Revere
Chelsea
Winthrop
Somerville
Cambridge
Waltham
Belmont
Watertown
Weston
Newton
Boston
Brookline
Wellesley
Needham
Dedham
Milton
Quincy
Weymouth
Hingham
Braintree
Randolph
Holbrook
Rockland
Stoughton
Avon
Brockton
Whitman
Abington
Hanson
North Cohasset
Hull
Nahant
Bedford
West Bedford

NORTH END
WEST END
BEACON HILL
CHINATOWN
FINANCIAL DISTRICT
SOUTH BOSTON
CHARLESTOWN

Boston Harbor
Quincy Bay
Hingham Bay
Nantasket Beach

Map Scale
1 : 578,000

1 inch = 9.1 miles
or 14.6 kilometers

MI   5   10   15
KM   5   10   15

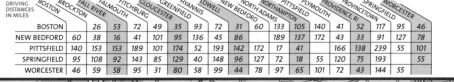

DRIVING DISTANCES IN MILES

	BOSTON	BROCKTON	FALL RIVER	FALMOUTH	FITCHBURG	GLOUCESTER	GREENFIELD	HYANNIS	LOWELL	NEW BEDFORD	NORTH ADAMS	NORTHAMPTON	PITTSFIELD	PLYMOUTH	PROVIDENCE RI	PROVINCETOWN	SPRINGFIELD	WORCESTER
BOSTON		26	53	72	49	35	93	72	31	60	133	105	140	41	52	117	95	46
NEW BEDFORD	60	38	16	41	101	95	136	45	86		189	137	172	43	33	91	127	78
PITTSFIELD	140	153	153	189	101	174	52	193	142	172	17	41		166	138	239	57	101
SPRINGFIELD	95	108	92	143	85	129	40	148	96	127	50	18	55	120	75	193		55
WORCESTER	46	59	58	95	31	80	58	99	44	78	97	65	101	72	43	144	55	

Map Scale
1 : 1,283,000

1 inch = 20.3 miles
or 32.7 kilometers

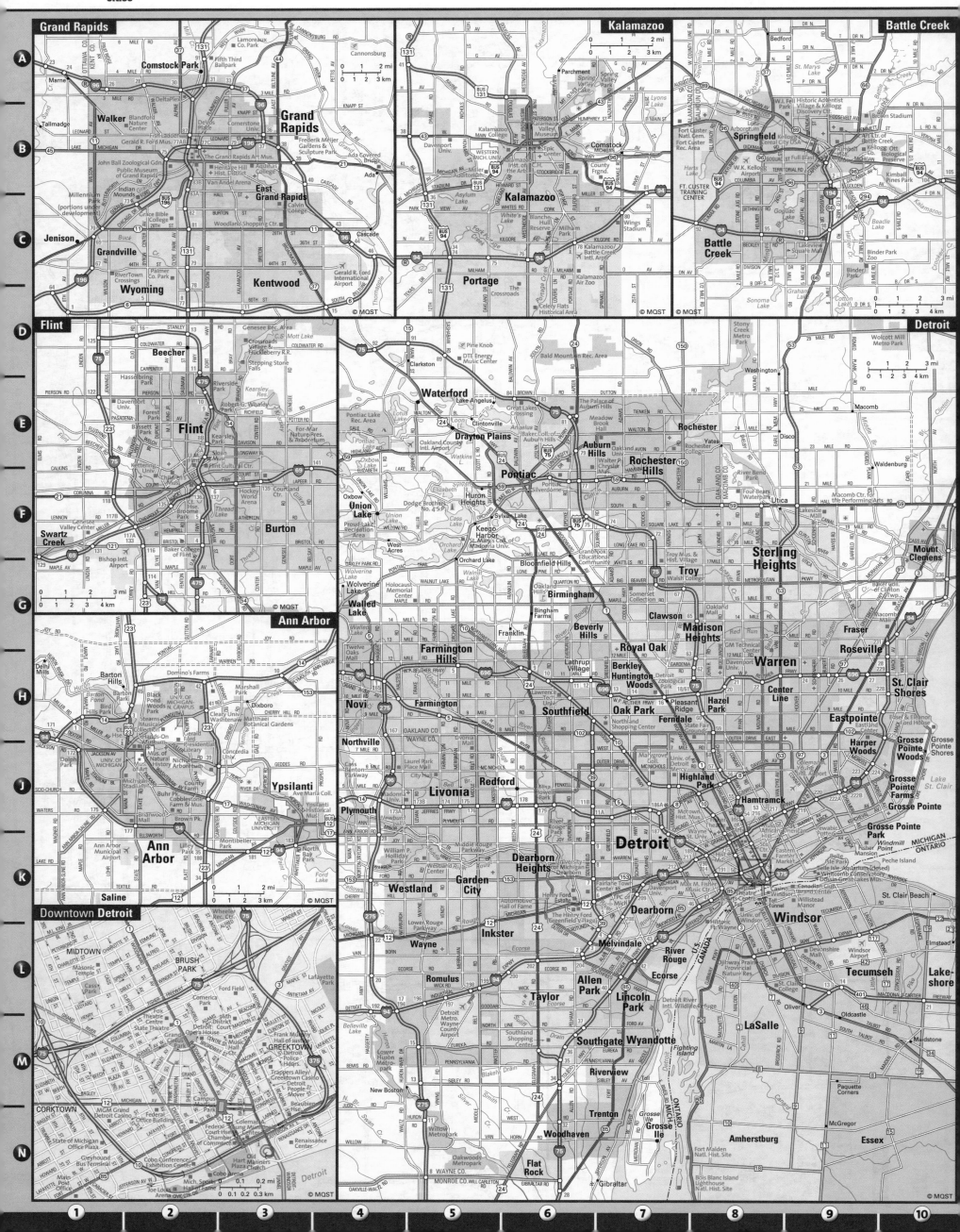

DRIVING DISTANCES IN MILES	ALBERT LEA	BEMIDJI	BRAINERD	DULUTH	FERGUS FALLS	GRAND FORKS ND	INTERNATIONAL FALLS	MANKATO	MARSHALL	MINNEAPOLIS	MOORHEAD	ROCHESTER	ST. CLOUD	ST. PAUL	VIRGINIA	WILLMAR	WINONA	WORTHINGTON
DULUTH	251	153	116		210	264	157	239	274	158	257	239	149	154	61	206	216	362
MINNEAPOLIS	96	225	129	158	176	312	290	78	148		230	88	64	10	193	92	120	207
MOORHEAD	325	133	141	257	55	80	242	294	220	230		317	172	239		168	351	298
ROCHESTER	62	311	215	239	262	399	371	80	185	88	317		151	80	229	177	51	174
ST. CLOUD	159	157	62	149	117	254	251	128	131	64	172	151		73	184	63	185	201

Map Scale
1 : 1,735,000

1 inch = 27.4 miles
or 44.1 kilometers

DRIVING DISTANCES IN MILES	BILOXI	COLUMBUS	GREENVILLE	HATTIESBURG	JACKSON	MEMPHIS TN	MERIDIAN	NATCHEZ	NEW ORLEANS LA	TUPELO	VICKSBURG	WINONA
BILOXI		262	297	82	172	379	171	231	93	317	214	262
GREENVILLE	297	164		215	125	148	216	157	310	172	89	82
JACKSON	172	153	125	90		211	91	102	185	175	42	94
MERIDIAN	171	91	216	89	91	234		194	201	146	133	113
TUPELO	317	66	172	235	175	109	146	269	347		213	99

Kansas City

Downtown Kansas City

St Joseph

Joplin

Branson

Springfield

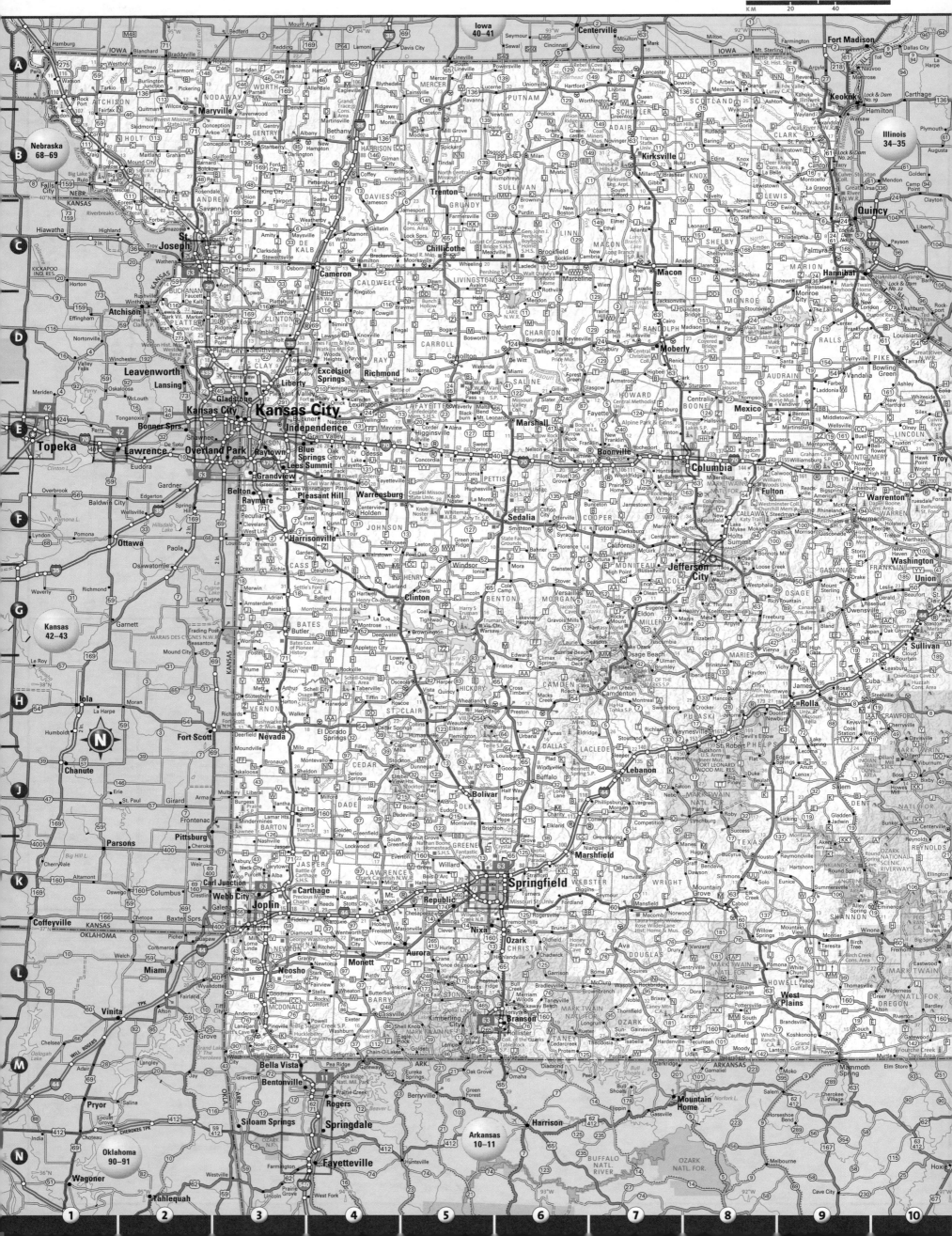

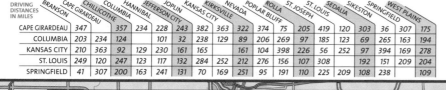

	BRANSON	CAPE GIRARDEAU	CHILLICOTHE	COLUMBIA	HANNIBAL	JEFFERSON CITY	JOPLIN	KANSAS CITY	KIRKSVILLE	NEVADA	POPLAR BLUFF	ROLLA	ST. JOSEPH	ST. LOUIS	SEDALIA	SIKESTON	SPRINGFIELD	WEST PLAINS
CAPE GIRARDEAU	347		357	234	228	243	382	363	322	374	75	205	419	120	303	36	307	175
COLUMBIA	203	234	124		101	32	238	129	89	206	269	97	185	123	69	265	163	194
KANSAS CITY	210	363	92	129	230	161	165		161	104	398	226	56	252	97	394	169	278
ST. LOUIS	249	120	247	123	117	132	284	252	212	276	156	107	308		192	151	209	204
SPRINGFIELD	41	307	200	163	241	131	70	169	251	95	191	110	225	209	108	238		109

Map Scale
1 : 1,436,000

1 inch = 22.7 miles
or 36.5 kilometers

© MapQuest

DRIVING DISTANCES IN MILES	ALLIANCE	BEATRICE	CHADRON	COLUMBUS	GRAND ISLAND	HASTINGS	KEARNEY	LINCOLN	MC COOK	NEBRASKA CITY	NORFOLK	NORTH PLATTE	OGALLALA	OMAHA	O'NEILL	SCOTTSBLUFF	SOUTH SIOUX CITY	VALENTINE
GRAND ISLAND	317	135	373	64		23	49	95	147	144	105	143	196	150	111	318	179	210
LINCOLN	397	40	453	77	95	102	129		226	49	119	223	275	58	207	397	154	302
NORTH PLATTE	174	262	230	207	143	150	98	223	67	271	248		53	278	203	175	374	131
OMAHA	452	97	508	84	150	157	184	58	281	50	115	278	330		188	452	99	298
SCOTTSBLUFF	55	437	96	382	318	325	273	397	242	446	423	175	122	452	324		549	214

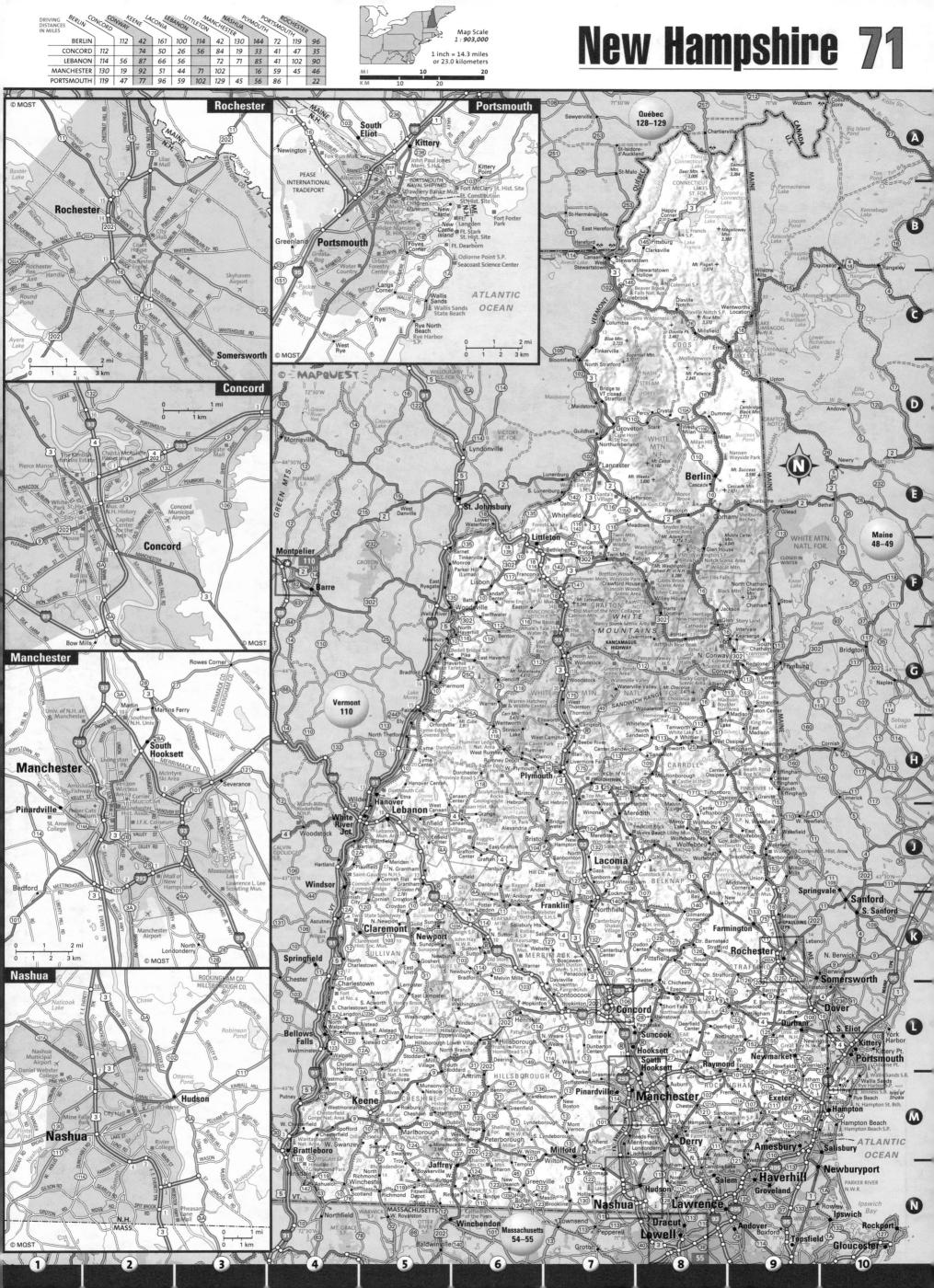

DRIVING DISTANCES IN MILES	BERLIN	CONCORD	CONWAY	KEENE	LACONIA	LEBANON	LITTLETON	MANCHESTER	NASHUA	PLYMOUTH	PORTSMOUTH	ROCHESTER
BERLIN		112	42	161	100	114	42	130	144	72	119	96
CONCORD	112		74	50	26	56	84	19	33	41	47	35
LEBANON	114	56	87	66	56		72	71	85	41	102	90
MANCHESTER	130	19	92	51	44	71	102		16	59	45	46
PORTSMOUTH	119	47	77	96	59	102	129	45	56	86		22

Map Scale 1 : 903,000

1 inch = 14.3 miles or 23.0 kilometers

Map Scale
1 : 533,000

1 inch = 8.4 miles
or 13.5 kilometers

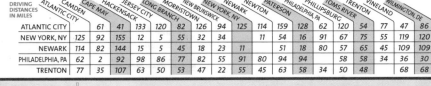

New Jersey 73

DRIVING DISTANCES IN MILES	CAMDEN	CAPE MAY	HACKENSACK	JERSEY CITY	LONG BRANCH	MORRISTOWN	NEW BRUNSWICK	NEW YORK, NY	NEWARK	NEWTON	PATERSON	PHILADELPHIA, PA	PHILLIPSBURG	TOMS RIVER	TRENTON	VINELAND	WILMINGTON, DE
ATLANTIC CITY	61	41	133	120	82	126	94	125	114	159	128	62	120	54	77	47	86
NEW YORK, NY	125	92	155	12	5	55	32	34	11	11	54	16	91	67	75	55	119	120
NEWARK	114	82	144	15	5	45	18	23	11	51	18	80	57	65	45	109	109
PHILADELPHIA, PA	62	2	92	98	86	77	82	55	91	80	94	94	58	58	34	36	30
TRENTON	77	35	107	63	50	53	47	22	55	45	63	58	34	50	48	68	68

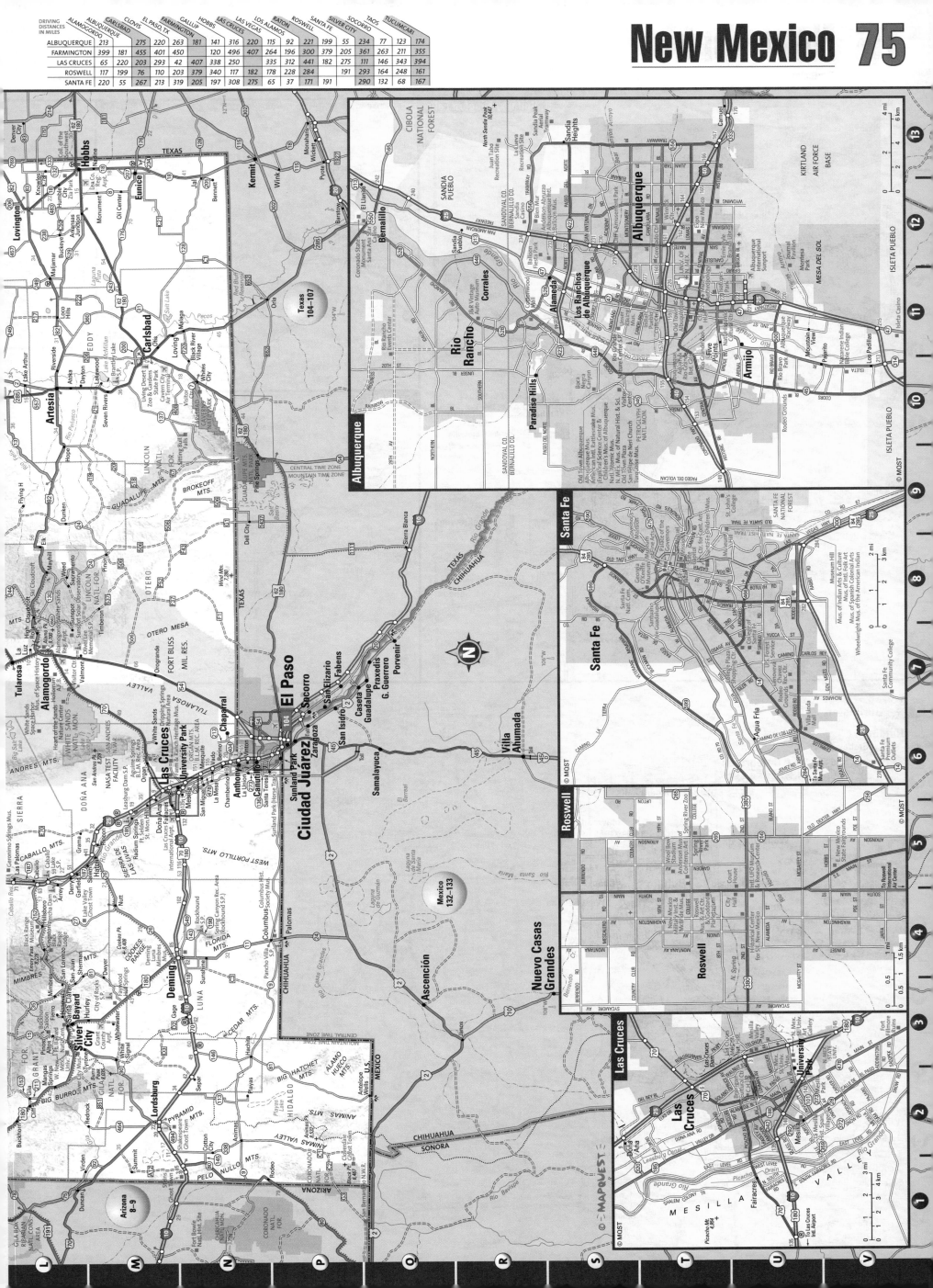

DRIVING DISTANCES IN MILES

	ALAMOGORDO	ALBUQUERQUE	CARLSBAD	CLOVIS	EL PASO, TX	FARMINGTON	GALLUP	HOBBS	LAS CRUCES	LAS VEGAS	LOS ALAMOS	RATON	ROSWELL	SANTA FE	SILVER CITY	SOCORRO	TAOS	TUCUMCARI
ALBUQUERQUE	213		275	220	263	181	141	316	220	115	92	221	199	55	234	77	123	174
FARMINGTON	399	181	455	401	450		120	496	407	264	196	300	379	205	361	263	211	355
LAS CRUCES	65	220	203	293	42	407	338	250		335	312	441	182	275	111	146	343	394
ROSWELL	117	199	76	110	203	379	340	117	182	178	228	284		191	293	164	248	161
SANTA FE	220	55	267	213	319	205	197	308	275	65	37	171	191		290	132	68	167

Map Scale
1 : 574,000
1 inch = 9.1 miles
or 14.6 kilometers

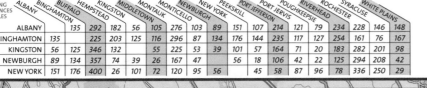

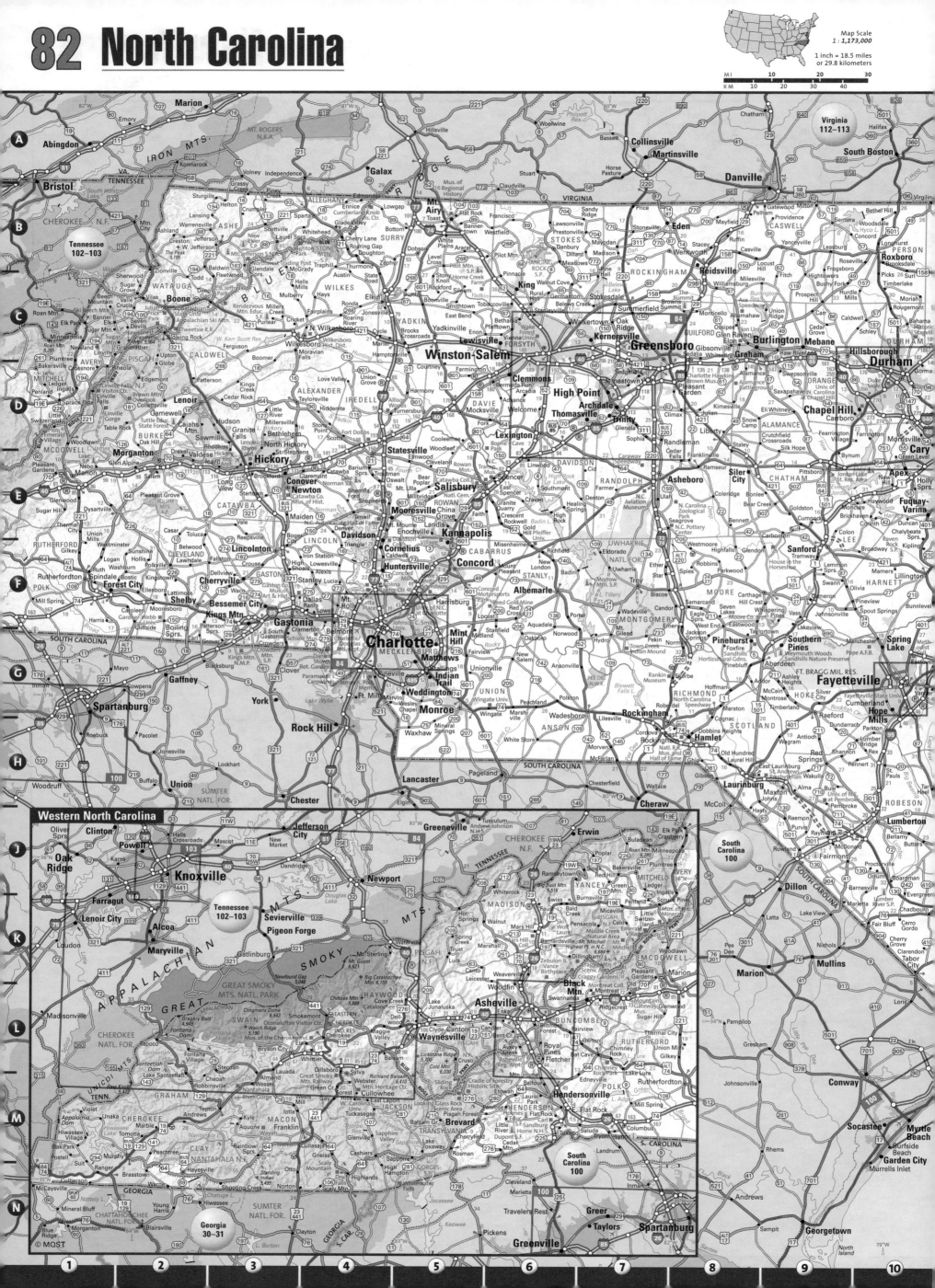

Map Scale
1 : 1,173,000
1 inch = 18.5 miles
or 29.8 kilometers

DRIVING DISTANCES IN MILES	ASHEVILLE	BOONE	CHARLOTTE	DURHAM	ELIZABETH CITY	FAYETTEVILLE	GREENSBORO	GREENVILLE	HICKORY	JACKSONVILLE	KINSTON	MOREHEAD CITY	NAGS HEAD	RALEIGH	ROCKY MOUNT	ROCKINGHAM	WILMINGTON	WINSTON-SALEM
ASHEVILLE		198	116	224	404	264	176	324	78	354	316	383	444	242	190	297	368	146
CHARLOTTE	116	95		139	319	139	91	239	48	269	232	298	359	158	74	213	205	79
GREENSBORO	176	117	91	49	228	90		148	98	179	141	207	268	83	122	193	30	
RALEIGH	242	183	158	24	160	62	67	80	164	113	76	142	200		96	54	127	96
WILMINGTON	368	309	205	150	211	92	193	123	290	52	93	95	241	127	131	153		222

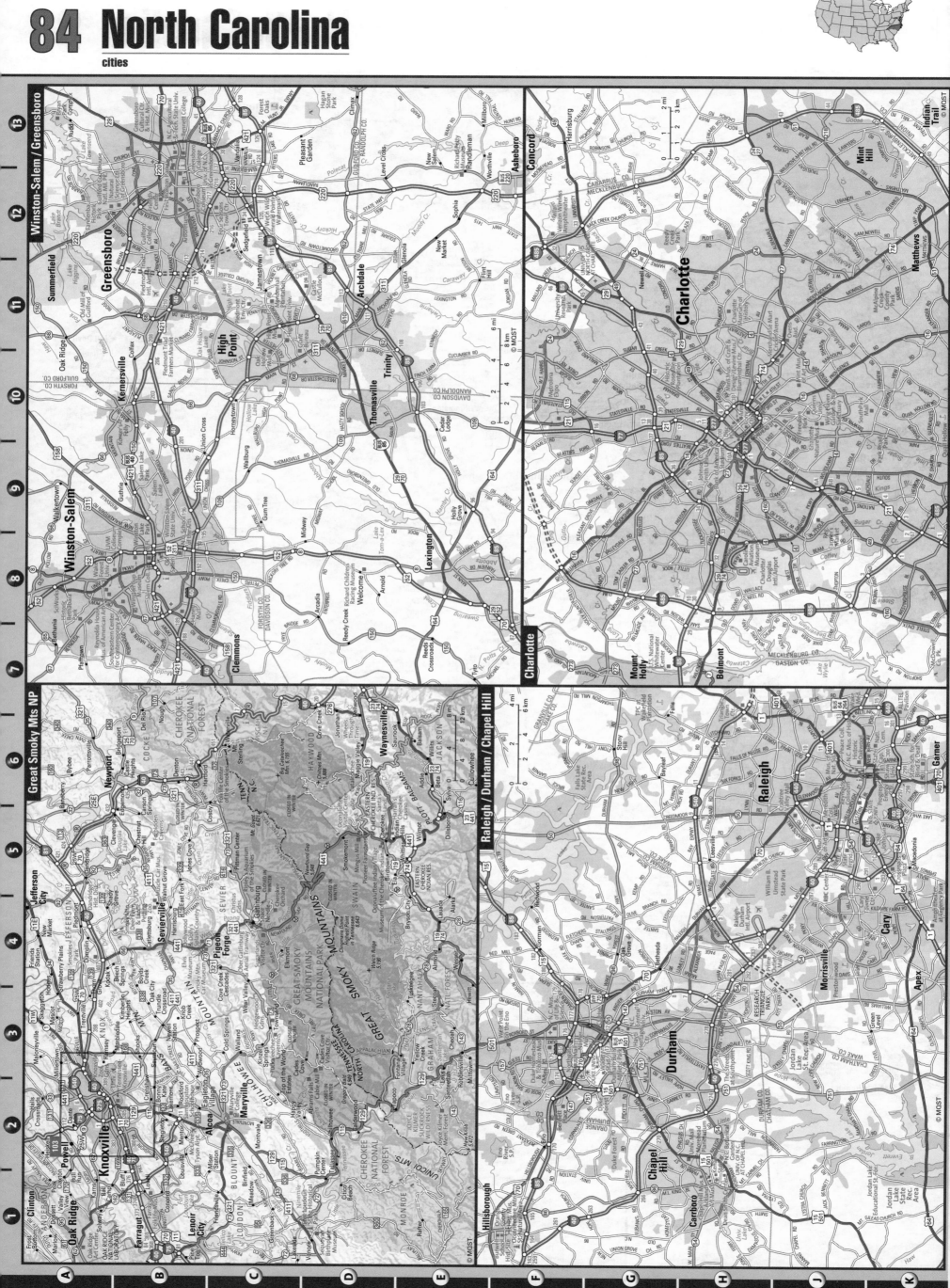

DRIVING DISTANCES IN MILES

	BISMARCK	DEVILS LAKE	DICKINSON	FARGO	GRAND FORKS	JAMESTOWN	MINOT	PEMBINA	RUGBY	VALLEY CITY	WAHPETON	WILLISTON
BISMARCK		186	97	199	274	105	116	347	153	141	249	229
DICKINSON	97	278		291	367	197	178	440	245	234	341	133
FARGO	199	163	291		79	268	152	221	58	55	424
GRAND FORKS	274	91	367	79		173	212	77	148	133	130	340
MINOT	116	122	178	268	212	171		238	64	210	318	128

Map Scale
1 : 1,832,000

1 inch = 28.9 miles
or 46.5 kilometers

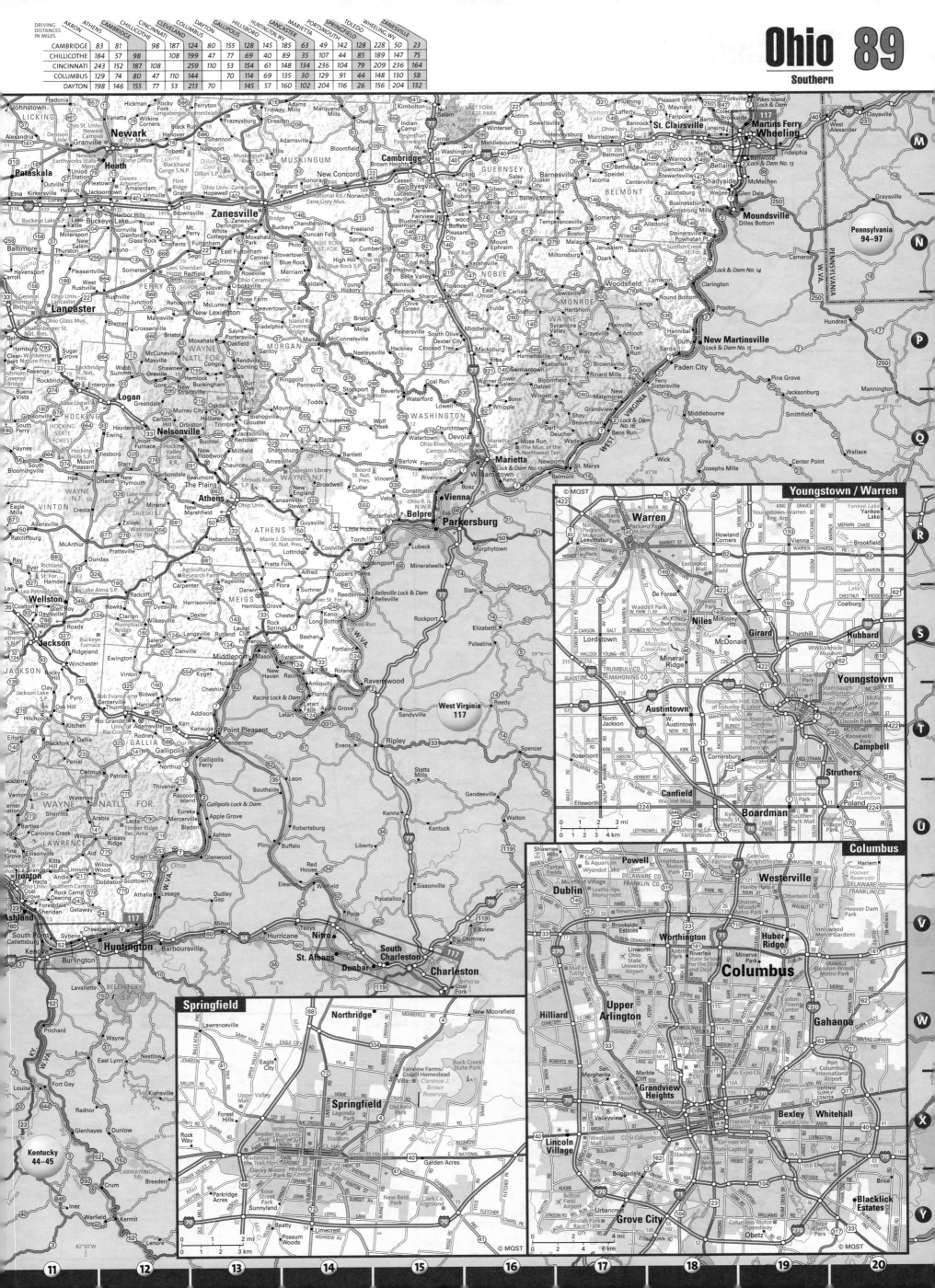

Pennsylvania 94–97

Kentucky 44–45

West Virginia 117

Map Scale
1 : 1,527,000

1 inch = 24.1 miles
or 38.8 kilometers

DRIVING DISTANCES IN MILES	ARDMORE	BARTLESVILLE	DALLAS, TX	DURANT	ELK CITY	ENID	FORT SMITH, AR	GUYMON	HUGO	LAWTON	MC ALESTER	MIAMI	MUSKOGEE	OKLAHOMA CITY	PONCA CITY	STILLWATER	TULSA	WOODWARD
ENID	183	141	292	238	148		242	219	282	142	210	207	168	84	69	66	117	88
LAWTON	103	243	197	158	115	142	270	297	224		211	283	223	85	192	152	194	175
MC ALESTER	117	141	169	77	245	210	114	407	75	211		160	68	133	186	154	93	276
OKLAHOMA CITY	99	157	209	154	112	84	191	274	205	85	133	198	144		107	67	109	143
TULSA	206	48	259	168	221	117	125	336	165	194	93	91	52	109	93	71		205

Map Scale
1 : 758,000

1 inch = 12.0 miles
or 19.3 kilometers

MI 10 20
KM 10 20 30

State College

Altoona

Erie

New York 76-79

Ohio 86-89

LAKE ERIE

CANADA
UNITED STATES

ONTARIO

NEW YORK

OHIO

N

© MapQuest
© MOST

DRIVING DISTANCES IN MILES	ALLENTOWN	ALTOONA	CHAMBERSBURG	ERIE	HARRISBURG	INDIANA	JOHNSTOWN	LEWISTOWN	MEADVILLE	NEW CASTLE	PHILADELPHIA	PITTSBURGH	SCRANTON	STATE COLLEGE	UNIONTOWN	WARREN	WASHINGTON	WILLIAMSPORT
ALTOONA	218		95	205	140	55	48	71	168	129	241	99	185	40	109	147	123	99
ERIE	361	205	282		298	150	195	242	49	71	405	130	317	210	183	66	153	259
HARRISBURG	82	140	54	298		179	138	58	261	250	109	205	119	88	200	224	213	83
PITTSBURGH	284	99	160	126	205	56	73	155	88	49	306		301	139	48	145	30	215
STATE COLLEGE	165	40	105	210	88	95	87	32	172	167	195	139	149		148	136	163	63

Philadelphia

Downtown Philadelphia

Pittsburgh

Downtown Pittsburgh

DRIVING DISTANCES IN MILES

	BOSTON, MA	BRISTOL	EAST GREENWICH	FALL RIVER, MA	HOPE VALLEY	KINGSTON	NEWPORT	PROVIDENCE	WARWICK	WESTERLY	WICKFORD	WOONSOCKET
NEWPORT	73	14	20	20	28	17		33	27	41	13	46
PROVIDENCE	52	16	12	17	30	29	33		12	46	20	16
WARWICK	63	25	6	24	23	27	12			40	14	26
WESTERLY	97	60	41	61	17	26	41	46	40		34	59
WOONSOCKET	52	30	26	31	43	42	46	16	26	59	33	

Map Scale 1 : 359,000

1 inch = 5.7 miles or 9.2 kilometers

Providence

Newport

Connecticut 22–23

Massachusetts 54–55

ATLANTIC OCEAN

© MapQuest

Map Scale
1 : 1,431,000

1 inch = 22.6 miles
or 36.4 kilometers

DRIVING DISTANCES IN MILES	AUGUSTA, GA	CHARLOTTE, NC	CHARLESTON	COLUMBIA	FLORENCE	GREENVILLE	HILTON HEAD ISLAND	MYRTLE BEACH	ROCK HILL	SAVANNAH, GA	SPARTANBURG	SUMTER
CHARLESTON	142	204		110	127	205	95	92	183	107	200	100
COLUMBIA	70	91	110		80	97	152	146	70	159	92	45
FLORENCE	147	107	127	80		174	170	66	115	176	169	39
GREENVILLE	110	96	205	97	174		248	241	88	255	30	142
MYRTLE BEACH	213	173	92	146	66	241	190		181	197	235	93

DRIVING DISTANCES IN MILES	ABERDEEN	BELLE FOURCHE	BROOKINGS	HOT SPRINGS	HURON	MITCHELL	MOBRIDGE	PIERRE	RAPID CITY	SIOUX FALLS	WATERTOWN	YANKTON
ABERDEEN		310	150	412	90	146	99	160	357	204	98	231
PIERRE	160	247	188	247	115	155	107		193	226	189	240
RAPID CITY	357	56	390	56	313	275	243	193		346	436	360
SIOUX FALLS	204	401	57	401	127	73	303	226	346		103	80
WATERTOWN	98	360	49	490	86	162	196	189	436	103		179

Map Scale
1 : 2,057,000

1 inch = 32.5 miles
or 52.3 kilometers

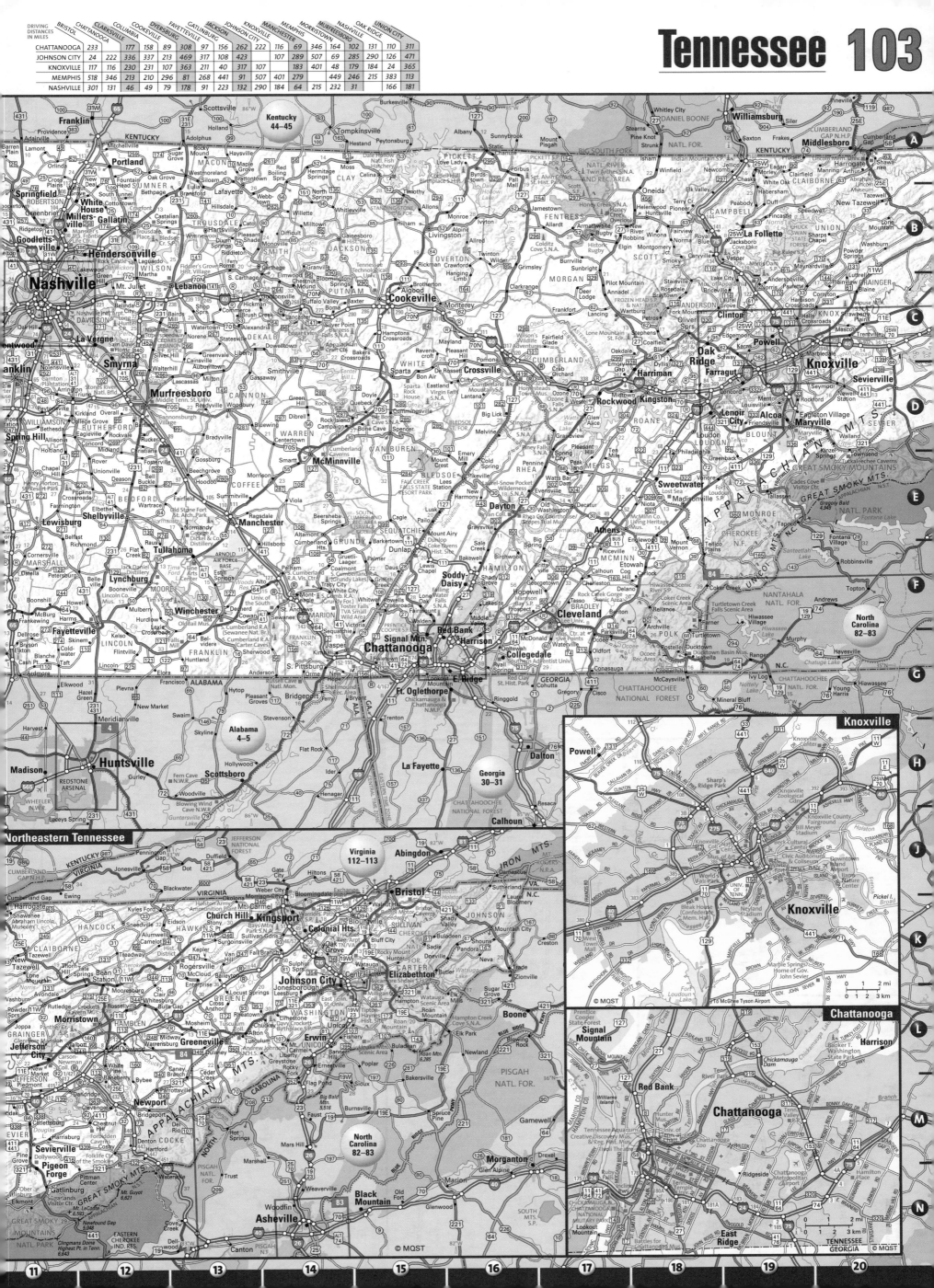

DRIVING DISTANCES IN MILES

	BRISTOL	CHATTANOOGA	CLARKSVILLE	COLUMBIA	COOKEVILLE	DYERSBURG	FAYETTEVILLE	GATLINBURG	JACKSON	JOHNSON CITY	KNOXVILLE	MANCHESTER	MEMPHIS	MORRISTOWN	MURFREESBORO	NASHVILLE	OAK RIDGE	UNION CITY
CHATTANOOGA	233		177	158	89	308	97	156	262	222	116	69	346	164	102	131	110	311
JOHNSON CITY	24	222	336	337	213	469	317	108	423		107	289	507	69	285	290	126	471
KNOXVILLE	117	116	230	231	107	363	211	40	317	107		183	401	48	179	184	24	365
MEMPHIS	518	346	213	210	296	81	268	441	91	507	401	279		449	246	215	383	113
NASHVILLE	301	131	46	49	79	178	91	223	132	290	184	64	215	232	31		166	181

Map Scale
1 : 1,982,000

1 inch = 31.3 miles
or 50.4 kilometers

DRIVING DISTANCES IN MILES

	ABILENE	ALPINE	AMARILLO	BIG BEND N.P.	BIG SPRING	CHILDRESS	DALHART	DALLAS	DEL RIO	EL PASO	FORT STOCKTON	LUBBOCK	ODESSA	PECOS	SAN ANGELO	SAN ANTONIO	VAN HORN	WICHITA FALLS
AMARILLO	290	414		472	230	118	87	470	462	438	349	124	266	340	308	513	427	228
EL PASO	459	232	438	329	347	558	420	647	425		241	341	341	142	217	185	389	303	596
LUBBOCK	166	291	124	349	106	144	211	354	338	341	226		142	217	185	389	303	207
ODESSA	176	151	266	209	65	276	353	364	246	285	86	142		76	134	342	163	314
SAN ANGELO	91	230	308	287	87	238	395	265	156	416	164	185	134	208		208	295	232

Map Scale
1 : 1,982,000

1 inch = 31.3 miles
or 50.4 kilometers

DRIVING DISTANCES IN MILES	ABILENE	AUSTIN	BEAUMONT	BROWNSVILLE	COLLEGE STATION	CORPUS CHRISTI	DALLAS	DEL RIO	FORT WORTH	HOUSTON	LAREDO	MC ALLEN	SAN ANGELO	SAN ANTONIO	TEXARKANA	TYLER	WACO	WICHITA FALLS
AUSTIN	217		250	350	108	217	195	229	187	166	238	313	207	78	375	229	105	301
CORPUS CHRISTI	411	217	293	157	254		411	272	403	211	141	152	362	147	591	445	321	517
DALLAS	191	195	323	544	184	411		422	32	241	432	507	265	271	179	100	94	141
HOUSTON	425	166	84	351	106	211	241	349	275		355	346	410	200	290	202	203	382
SAN ANTONIO	258	78	284	279	171	147	271	152	264	200	157	243	208		452	306	182	378

Downtown San Antonio

Corpus Christi

San Antonio

Laredo

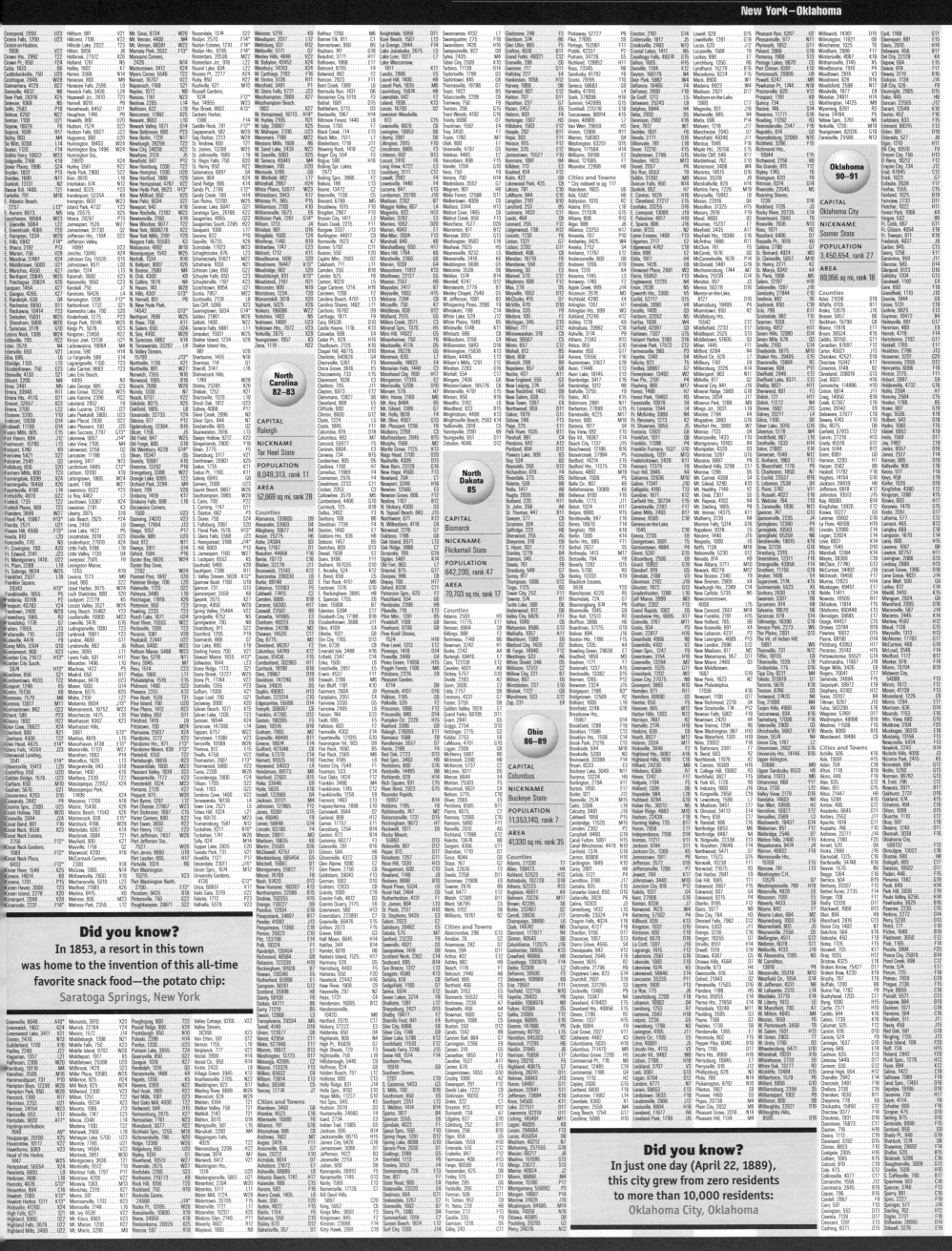

Oregon 92–93

CAPITAL
Salem

NICKNAME
Beaver State

POPULATION
3,421,399, rank 28

AREA
97,073 sq mi, rank 10

Counties

Cities and Towns

Pennsylvania 94–97

CAPITAL
Harrisburg

NICKNAME
Keystone State

POPULATION
12,281,054, rank 6

AREA
45,308 sq mi, rank 33

Counties

Cities and Towns

Did you know?
The deepest lake in the United States is found in the bowl-shaped depression atop an extinct Oregon volcano:
Crater Lake

Rhode Island 99

CAPITAL
Providence

NICKNAME
Ocean State

POPULATION
1,048,319, rank 43

AREA
1,212 sq mi, rank 50

Counties

Cities and Towns

South Carolina 100

CAPITAL
Columbia

NICKNAME
Palmetto State

POPULATION
4,012,012, rank 26

AREA
31,113 sq mi, rank 40

Counties

Cities and Towns

South Dakota 101

CAPITAL
Pierre

NICKNAME
Mount Rushmore State

POPULATION
754,844, rank 46

AREA
77,116 sq mi, rank 16

Counties

Cities and Towns

Did you know?
The outside of an exhibition building in South Dakota is decorated every year with murals made of multicolored corn, barley, and other grains:
The Corn Palace in Mitchell

Tennessee 102–103

CAPITAL
Nashville

NICKNAME
Volunteer State

POPULATION
5,689,283, rank 16

AREA
42,144 sq mi, rank 34

Counties

Cities and Towns

Texas 104–107

CAPITAL
Austin

NICKNAME
Lone Star State

POPULATION
20,851,820, rank 2

AREA
266,807 sq mi, rank 2

Counties

Cities and Towns

Did you know?
In 1978, Ben and Jerry started making ice cream in a renovated garage in this northern town:
Burlington, Vermont

Did you know?
Long frequented by Native Americans, and later surveyed by George Washington, this site became the first public spa in the U.S.:
Berkeley Springs, West Virginia

Wyoming 120

CAPITAL
Cheyenne

NICKNAME
Equality State

POPULATION
493,782, rank 50

AREA
97,809 sq mi, rank 9

Canada

Alberta 123
CAPITAL Edmonton
POPULATION 2,974,807, rank 4
AREA 255,541 sq mi, rank 6

British Columbia 122
CAPITAL Victoria
POPULATION 3,907,738, rank 3
AREA 364,764 sq mi, rank 5

Manitoba 125
CAPITAL Winnipeg
POPULATION 1,119,583, rank 5
AREA 250,116 sq mi, rank 8

New Brunswick 130
CAPITAL Fredericton
POPULATION 729,498, rank 8
AREA 28,150 sq mi, rank 11

Newfoundland and Labrador 131
CAPITAL St. John's
POPULATION 512,930, rank 9
AREA 156,453 sq mi, rank 10

Northwest Territories 121
CAPITAL Yellowknife
POPULATION 37,360, rank 11
AREA 519,734 sq mi (est.), rank 3

Nunavut 121
CAPITAL Iqaluit
POPULATION 26,745, rank 13
AREA 808,185 sq mi, rank 1

Nova Scotia 130–131
CAPITAL Halifax
POPULATION 908,007, rank 7
AREA 21,345 sq mi, rank 12

Ontario 126–127
CAPITAL Toronto
POPULATION 11,410,046, rank 1
AREA 415,598 sq mi, rank 4

Prince Edward Island 130–131
CAPITAL Charlottetown
POPULATION 135,294, rank 10
AREA 2,185 sq mi, rank 13

Québec 128–129
CAPITAL Québec
POPULATION 7,237,479, rank 2
AREA 595,391 sq mi, rank 2

Saskatchewan 124
CAPITAL Regina
POPULATION 978,933, rank 6
AREA 251,366 sq mi, rank 7

Yukon Territory 121
CAPITAL Whitehorse
POPULATION 28,674, rank 12
AREA 186,272 sq mi, rank 9

Mexico

Mexico 132–133
CAPITAL México
POPULATION 95,772,462
AREA 756,066 sq mi

Puerto Rico

Puerto Rico 134
CAPITAL San Juan
POPULATION 3,808,610
AREA 3,435 sq mi

Interstate Route
Other Route
206 Distance in Miles
4:15 Approximate Travel Time
● Miami City on Mileage Chart (page 144)
● Fort Pierce Other City

© MAPQUEST

Distances and driving times may vary depending on actual
route traveled and driving conditions.

Distances in chart are in miles.
To convert miles to kilometers,
multiply the distance in miles
by 1.609.

Example:
New York, NY to Boston, MA
= 215 miles or 346 kilometers
(215 x 1.609)

© MAPQUEST

The chart lists driving distances (in miles) between the following cities, arranged as a triangular mileage matrix:

Albany, NY · Albuquerque, NM · Amarillo, TX · Atlanta, GA · Baltimore, MD · Billings, MT · Birmingham, AL · Bismarck, ND · Boise, ID · Boston, MA · Buffalo, NY · Burlington, VT · Charleston, SC · Charleston, WV · Charlotte, NC · Cheyenne, WY · Chicago, IL · Cincinnati, OH · Cleveland, OH · Columbus, OH · Dallas, TX · Denver, CO · Des Moines, IA · Detroit, MI · El Paso, TX · Hartford, CT · Houston, TX · Indianapolis, IN · Jackson, MS · Jacksonville, FL · Kansas City, MO · Las Vegas, NV · Little Rock, AR · Los Angeles, CA · Louisville, KY · Memphis, TN · Miami, FL · Milwaukee, WI · Minneapolis, MN · Mobile, AL · Montréal, QC · Nashville, TN · New Orleans, LA · New York, NY · Norfolk, VA · Oklahoma City, OK · Omaha, NE · Orlando, FL · Philadelphia, PA · Phoenix, AZ · Pittsburgh, PA · Portland, ME · Portland, OR · Raleigh, NC · Rapid City, SD · Reno, NV · Richmond, VA · St. Louis, MO · Salt Lake City, UT · San Antonio, TX · San Diego, CA · San Francisco, CA · Seattle, WA · Tampa, FL · Toronto, ON · Vancouver, BC · Washington, DC · Wichita, KS